# DESIGN D&T MAKE IT !

# electronic
# products
## revised edition

Dave Mawson ■ Paul Bell ■ Philip Poole ■ Tristram Shepard

First edition published in 1996 by Stanley Thornes (Publishers) Ltd
Second edition published in 2001 by:

Nelson Thornes Ltd
Delta Place
27 Bath Road
CHELTENHAM
GL53 7TH
United Kingdom

01 02 03 04 05 / 10 9 8 7 6 5 4 3 2 1

A catalogue record for this book is available from the British Library

ISBN 0 7487 6079 2

Designed and typeset by Carla Turchini
Picture research by Jennie Karrach and johnbailey@axonimages.com
Artwork by Andrew Loft, Hardlines, Mark Dunn, Tristram Shepard
Printed and Bound in Italy by Canale

Thanks are due to Andy Biggs, Richard Calrert, Roy Ballam, Russ Jones and Jet Mayor for their contributions to the revised edition.

The authors would like to acknowledge the influence of the following books and magazines and recommend them as sources of further information for teachers and pupils:
*CMOS Cookbook*, Don Lancaster, Sams (1986)
*Electronics for Today and Tomorrow*, Tom Duncan, John Murray (1985)
*GCSE Electronics*, Tom Duncan, John Murray (1989)
*Practical Electronics for GCSE*, Owen Bishop, John Murray (1989)
*Electronics through Systems*, Mike Geddes, The Institution of Electrical Engineers (1983)
*Electronics / Control / Manufacturing*, Technology Enhancement Programme (1994)
*GCSE Technology: Electronics*, Steve Rich and Anthony Edwards, Stanley Thornes (Publishers) Ltd (1990)
*Physics For You*, Keith Johnson, Stanley Thornes (Publishers) Ltd (1996)
*Design and Make It! Resistant Materials Technology / Graphic Products*, Nelson Thornes Ltd (2001)
*GCSE Craft Design and Technology*, R Kimball, Thames/Hutchinson, (1987)
*Green Design*, Dorothy Mackenzie, Laurence King (1991)
*Mastering Manufacturing*, Gordon Mair, Macmillan (1993)
*Manufacturing By Design* (CAD software and curriculum materials), CBI, available from NCET
*New Designer*, (termly magazine for GCSE Design and Technology), Philip Allen Publishers (Tel. 01869 338652)
*Electronics Education* (Magazine), The Institution of Electrical Engineers

## Sources of Further Information
British Standards Institute, Marylands Avenue, Hemel Hempstead HP2 4SQ (Tel. 01442 230442)
Technology Enhancement Programme, Middlesex University, Trent Park, London N14 4XS (Tel. 0181 447 0342)
The Institution of Electrical Engineers, Savoy Place, London WC2R OBL. Publication Sales Dept, PO Box 96, Stevenage, Herts SG1 2SD (Tel. 01438 313311)

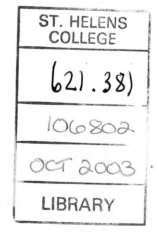

# Contents

# Project Three: Alarming Circuits

# Project Four: PCBs A ' Us

# Project Suggestions

# Introduction

*Welcome to* Design & Make: Electronic Products. *This book has been written to support you as you work through your GCSE course in Design and Technology. It will help guide you through the important stages of your coursework, and assist your preparation for the final examination paper.*

## Making it

Whatever your project, remember that the final realisation is particularly important. The quality of your final realisation counts for a high proportion of the marks. It is not enough to just hand in your design folio.

During your course you will need to develop your technical skills in using electronic components and your constructional skills using a range of materials. This is something you can't do just by reading a book! The best way is to watch carefully as different techniques and procedures are demonstrated to you, and practise them as often as possible.

The sequence of projects is progressive and therefore it will be difficult to work on the later projects without reference to the knowledge and skills associated with the previous ones.

References in the text will guide you to pages on which concepts are developed further.

## How to Use this Book

There are two main ways the book might be used.

1   Follow the four design and make projects in sequence over the whole course, including a selection of the suggested activities (i.e. focused practical tasks). This will ensure complete syllabus coverage. You do not necessarily need to take all of them as far as the production of a finished working product: discuss this with your teacher.
2   Undertake alternative projects to one or more of those provided and refer to those pages which cover the specific areas of knowledge and understanding defined in the examination syllabus and the KS4 National Curriculum.

## Contents

### Project Guide

The book begins with a coursework guide which summarises the design skills you will need for extended project work. Refer back to these pages throughout the course.

### The projects

Four projects are provided. These each contain a mixture of product analysis and development pages and knowledge and understanding pages which include short focused tasks. In each of the projects the development of one possible solution has been used as an on-going example. You could closely base your own work on this solution, but if you want to achieve higher marks you will need to try to come up with ideas of your own.

### Project suggestions

Finally, three outline project suggestions are provided. Refer to the Project Guide to help develop your ideas and to ensure you are covering and documenting your coursework in the way the examiners will be looking for.

## Long or short?

If you are following a short course, check with your teacher which sections of the book you do not need to cover.

### ■ ACTIVITY

Make sure that as part of your project folio you include evidence of having completed a number of short-term focused tasks, as suggested in the Activities.

### IN YOUR PROJECT

Use the 'In Your Project' paragraphs to help you think about how you could apply the content of the page to your current work.

### KEY POINTS

Use the 'Key Points' paragraphs to revise from when preparing for the final examination paper.

# Design Matters (1)

*What is Design and Technology, how has it changed, and why is it important?*

*As you develop your ideas for products you will often need to make important decisions about the social, moral, cultural and environmental impact of your product.*

## How does Design and Technology Affect our Lives?

Technology helps extend our natural capabilities. For example, it enables us to:

▷ travel further and faster

▷ send and receive messages across the world in an instant

▷ keep us warm in winter and cool in summer.

Designers help make new and existing technologies easy and more pleasant for people to use – they make them look and feel fun and fashionable, logical and safe to use. They also work out how to make them easy to produce in quantity, and cheap to manufacture and sell.

So Design and Technology is about improving people's lives by designing and making the things they need and want. But different people have different needs: what is beneficial to one person can cause a problem for someone else, or create undesirable damage to the environment.

A new design might enable someone to do something quicker, easier and cheaper, but might cause widespread unemployment or urban decay. It could also have a harmful impact on the delicate balance of nature.

As you develop your design ideas you will often need to make important decisions about the social, moral, cultural and environmental impact of your product.

## A brief history of electronic products

The history of electronics is comparatively short. Early developments were driven by medical research and the new communication devices of the early twentieth century. Many of the early products, such as radios and televisions, had circuits manipulated and controlled by thermionic valves. These were large components that had to warm up before they worked correctly.

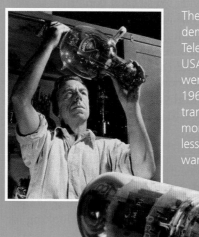

The transistor was first demonstrated by the Bell Telephone Laboratories in the USA in 1948, although they were not widely used until the 1960s. Compared to valves, transistors were more reliable, more durable, smaller, required less power and needed no warm-up time.

## Environmental Issues

We all need to be aware of the amount and use of energy and resources, as on our earth these are finite. The more we use up natural resources without replacing them, the fewer there are for future generations. Many products use plastics derived from petrochemicals that use non-replaceable energy and contributes to global warming.

## Social Needs

Good design can help bring people together. Designers need to be careful about creating products that might have the effect of isolating someone, or making them more vulnerable to crime in some way.

*Trevor Baylis's Clockwork radio is a good example of socially aware design. It is meant for use in Africa where batteries are extremely expensive. It is made in South Africa by a totally integrated workforce, which includes people with various physical handicaps.*

## Cultural Awareness

People from different cultures think and behave in different ways. What is acceptable to one culture may be confusing or insulting to another. For example, some religions are not allowed to watch TV or use computers. In others only very plain, undecorated products are acceptable. Colours and certain shapes can have very different meanings across the world.

## Moral Issues

Sometimes designers are asked to develop products that can cause harm to people or animals. Would you be willing to create an electronic product that could hurt someone or could also be used for criminal activity?

*Technology can invade people's privacy. Electronic surveillance equipment can be used to listen in to conversations and secretly take pictures. Warning of the potential implications of this, George Orwell used the phrase 'Big Brother is Watching You' in his novel '1984', written in 1948.*

Transistors are semi-conductors. They are made from materials which, in their pure form, neither conduct nor resist electricity. When modified with controlled amounts of impurities, however, they can be made to conduct or resist specific amounts of current.

Transistors can do four basic things to an electric current:
- detect its presence;
- convert it from AC to DC;
- amplify it;
- switch it on and off.

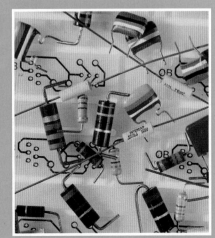

# Design Matters (2)

*Designing electronic products is a complex task. New designs must be:*
▷ *easy and comfortable to use;*
▷ *needed and wanted by enough people;*
▷ *suitable for manufacture.*

## Designing Electronic Products

Electronic products are found everywhere in our lives: controlling manufacturing processes, monitoring patients in hospital, recording business transactions in offices and entertaining us at home. Electronic products have transformed the way we live, and will continue to do so for the foreseeable future.

To design and make a successful 3D product you need to know what people need and want, and how materials and production technologies can be used to create it. You also need some skills in designing and making.

## Ergonomics

Designers need to make sure their products are a pleasure to own and use. This aspect of design is called **ergonomics**, and involves taking into consideration where the product will operate and how it will be used and operated. Things which are small and fiddly to open, or difficult to operate, can benefit from ergonomic study. You need to think carefully about things like:

▷ the weight and size of a product;

▷ the position of displays and controls;

▷ how the product is held and carried, and stored when not in use.

Sometimes this information is already available from books. If not, it may be necessary to set up a series of tests and experiments to obtain the data you need.

Military research and the space race of the 1960s pioneered today's familiar microchip technology. Printed circuit boards allowed transistors, resistors and capacitors to be made by etching them directly onto a sheet of semi-conducting material. This overcame the problem of wiring and soldering minute parts, and speeded up production significantly.

In recent years, the mechanical controls used in many domestic and industrial products have been replaced by electronic systems. Japan and other Pacific-rim countries lead the world in their ability to design, develop and mass produce cheap and reliable electronic components and products.

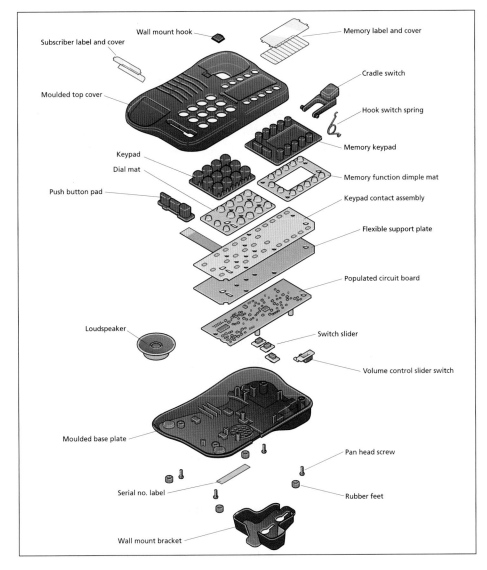

Wall mount hook

Subscriber label and cover

Memory label and cover

Moulded top cover

Cradle switch

Hook switch spring

Keypad

Dial mat

Memory keypad

Push button pad

Memory function dimple mat

Keypad contact assembly

Flexible support plate

Populated circuit board

Loudspeaker

Switch slider

Volume control slider switch

Moulded base plate

Pan head screw

Serial no. label

Rubber feet

Wall mount bracket

*Ergonomics and anthropometrics are essential when designing electronic products that people interact closely with*

## Anthropometrics

Anthropometrics is a term often used in connection with ergonomics. It refers to the measurement of the human body – how far we can see, the length of our legs, how much weight we can lift easily, the pressure we can apply with our hand, etc. Statistical data has been collected which gives these measurements as averages for males and females and for all ages from babies to elderly people. This information is important to help you check:

▷ if the intended user will find it easy to physically use the product (e.g. lifting, moving);

▷ whether any unusual skills are required;

▷ what accuracy of observation, decision and response is required;

▷ if instructions, information and control devices are arranged in the best way.

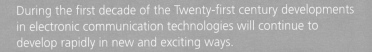

During the first decade of the Twenty-first century developments in electronic communication technologies will continue to develop rapidly in new and exciting ways.

The future of the design of electronic products lies in a further convergence of electronics and communication devices and new 'smart' materials that respond to their environments.

# Industrial Matters

*Good design involves creating something that works well and is satisfying to use. But to be successful a product also needs to be commercially viable.*

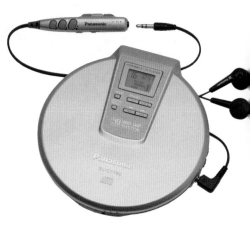

## Consumer Demands

Designers need to be clear about the gap or 'niche' in the market that their product is aiming to satisfy, and the sort of people it is aimed at.

People have a wide variety of needs and wants, and are prepared to spend different amounts of money to satisfy their desires. We don't just buy a personal stereo, for example. We want one in a particular price range which will have a specific range of functions, and looks the way we want it to look to reflect our life style. Manufacturers produce a range of models to satisfy different markets. Companies are keen to spot a gap in the market, i.e. a product model or variation which is not well supplied by other manufacturers.

## The Role of the Designer

One of the key skills of a designer is taking an existing component such an alarm circuit, working out how it will be housed safely and attractively, and how the various elements can be assembled quickly and easily.

Designers often have to design within considerable constraints. They rarely have a free choice of materials, components and production processes, and often have to work with what a manufacturer already has. Limitations may be imposed by the maximum size a machine can mould, an existing stock of ready-made electronic components and the existing skills of the workforce.

Some products are created with the prime intention of using materials and equipment which are being under-used during the decline in sales of a particular product.

## Design for Manufacture

To reduce production costs the design of a product should aim for simplicity in its making by using low-cost machinery and labour. This is discussed in more detail on pages 140–141.

## Design Failures

Sometimes products fail to sell in the marketplace. Maybe no-one wanted to buy the product, perhaps because there was a better or cheaper alternative. Or perhaps it quickly became known that it didn't work well, or was unreliable.

Maybe not enough money was invested in promotion, with the result that not enough people knew it was available, or manufacturing costs proved to be much higher than expected, with the result that no profit was made.

*Despite extensive publicity at the time, Sir Clive Sinclair's 'C5' vehicle of the early 1980's failed in the market place.*

*Personal stereos, portable CD players, minidisks and MP3 players all essentially do the same thing. However a wide range of models are made to cater for different markets. Identical electronic circuits, mechanisms and casings are often used across a range of devices to reduce production costs.*

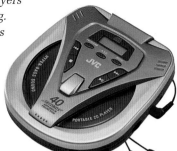

## Design for Profit

Products are designed and made to make life easier and more enjoyable, or to make a task or activity more efficient. However, along the way the people who create these products need to make a profit. The designer needs to do more than satisfy the needs of the market, and to consider the sorts of issues described on the previous page. They must also take into account the needs of the clients, manufacturers and retailers. The aim is to design and make products that are successful from everyone's point of view.

**Designers:**
- agree a brief with a client
- keep a notebook or log of all work done with dates so that time spent can be justified at the end of the project
- check that an identified need is real by examining the market for the product
- keep users' needs in mind at all times
- check existing ideas. Many designers re-style existing products to meet new markets because of changes in fashion, age, environment, materials, new technologies, etc.
- consider social, environmental and moral implications
- consider legal requirements
- set limits to the project to guide its development (design specification)
- produce workable ideas based on a thorough understanding of the brief
- design safe solutions
- suggest materials and production techniques after considering how many products are to be made
- produce working drawings for manufacturers to follow.

**Manufacturers need to:**
- make a profit on the products produced
- agree and set making limits for the product (manufacturing specification)
- develop marketing strategies
- understand and use appropriate production systems
- reduce parts and assembly time
- reduce labour and material costs
- apply safe working procedures to make safe products
- test products against specifications before distribution
- produce consistent results (quality assurance) by using quality control procedures
- understand and use product distribution systems
- be aware of legislation and consumer rights
- assume legal responsibility for product problems or failures.

**Retailers:**
- need to make a profit on the products sold
- consider the market for the product
- give consumers what they want, when they want it, at an acceptable price
- take account of consumers' legal rights
- take consumer complaints seriously
- continually review new products
- put in place a system to review and replace stock levels.

**Clients:**
- identify a need or opportunity and tell a designer what they want a product to do and who it's for (the brief)
- consider the possible market for the idea
- organise people, time and resources and raise finance for the project.

**Consumers/users expect the product to:**
- do the job it was designed for
- give pleasure in use
- have aesthetic appeal
- be safe for its purpose
- be of acceptable quality
- last for a reasonable lifetime
- offer value for money.

# Using ICT in Electronic Products

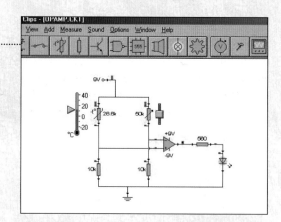

*ICT (Information and Communication Technology) is widely used in the design and production of products, as you will discover. You can considerably enhance your GCSE coursework with the effective use of ICT.*

##  Using ICT in your Work

To gain credit for using ICT you need to know when it is best to use a computer to help with your work. Sometimes it is easier to use ICT to help with parts of your coursework than to do it another way. On other occasions it can be far easier to write some notes on a piece of paper than use a computer – this saves you time and helps you to do the job more effectively.

Following are some ideas showing you how using ICT could enhance your coursework. Some can be used at more than one stage. You do not have to use all them!

## Identifying the Problem

The **Internet** could be used to search manufacturers' and retailers' web-sites for new products, indicating new product trends.

## Project Planning

A time chart can be produced showing the duration of the project and what you hope to achieve at each stage using a **word processor** or **DTP** program. Some programs allow you to produce a Gantt chart (see page 141).

## Investigation

▷ A questionnaire can be produced using a **word processor** or **DTP**. Results from a survey can be presented using a **spreadsheet** as a variety of graphs and charts.

▷ Use a **digital camera** to record visits and existing products

▷ The **Internet** can be used to perform literature searches and to communicate with other people around the world via **e-mail**.

## Search engines

To help you find the information you need on the Internet you can use a search engine. A search engine is a web-site that allows you to type in keywords for a specific subject. It then scans the Internet for web sites that match what you are looking for. Here are the addresses of some popular search engines:

**www.excite.co.uk**
**www.yahoo.co.uk**
**www.netscape.com**
**www.hotbot.co.uk**
**www.msn.co.uk**
**www.searchtheweb.com**

## E-mail

E-mail is a fast method of communicating with other people around the world. Text, photographs and computer files can be attached and shared. Some web-sites have e-mail addresses – you could try to contact experts to see if they could help with your coursework. It is important to be as specific as you possibly can, as these experts may be very busy people.

ICT

## Specification

A design or product specification can be written with a **word processor**. Visual images of the product, diagrams and other illustrations could also be added. Information can be easily modified at a later date.

## Developing Initial Ideas

Ideas for your product could be produced using a **graphics** program, **DTP** or **3D design** package. Colour variations can be applied to product drawings to test a design on its intended market before production.

Electronic circuits can be designed and simulated on screen to check their operation before they are made.

## Final Ideas and Production

A document showing the specification, images, production method and components can be **word processed**.

Parts lists and the costs of materials can be calculated and displayed using **spreadsheets**.

A detailed flow production diagram could be produced using a **DTP** program. Images could also be added to show important stages.

**Digital images** can be used in the production plan as a guide to show how the product should be assembled or to indicate its colour.

**Printed Circuit Board** production software can be used to produce PCB masks. More sophisticated software has an 'AutoRoute' facility that will produce a PCB mask directly from a circuit design program.

Pre-programmed **CAM** equipment could be used to replicate manufacture (see page 130).

## Project Presentation

Use **graphics packages** to prepare text and visual material for presentation panels. Charts showing numerical data can be quickly produced using a **spreadsheet**.

Use a **presentation** package, such as *PowerPoint* to communicate the main features of your design.

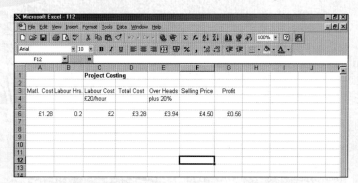

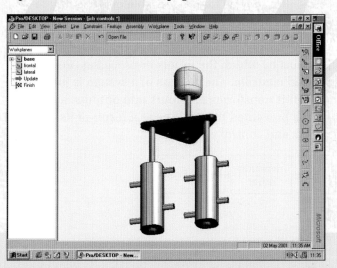

### IN YOUR PROJECT

▶ Use a CAD system to design a personalised logo on your project. Then use a computerised engraving machine to put this on your project.
▶ Use a CAD system to design the circuit for an electronic egg timer. Show how by adjusting component values the time period can be adjusted.

### KEY POINTS

● CAD will allow to design and check your designs before you start making.
● CAM will help you make your product; especially if you want several parts the same or have complex shapes.
● Generic software can be used to help present your work and product costs.

# Systems and Control

*Electronic products consist of a system made of components which can be controlled to produce a desired outcome. Meanwhile, the mass production of electronic products requires the design of complex manufacturing systems.*

## In Control

Control systems are an essential part of products such as cassette recorders, alarms and indicators, washing machines and cars. The systems are designed to ensure that the products behave as they were designed to:

▷ microwaves must control the energy delivered;
▷ washing machines need to fill and drain at the correct time during the washing cycle;
▷ alarms must only go off when they are supposed to.

At the heart of most control systems are microelectronic circuits designed to make decisions, time and count.

## Inputs, Outputs and Processes

All systems have **inputs** and **outputs** linked by a **processor**. The main purpose of a system is to act upon the inputs to produce the required outputs. Most systems have many different sorts of inputs and outputs. The first stage in analysing a system is to identify the inputs, the outputs and the transformation processes involved. It is useful to represent systems using **blocks**.

A good starting point for designing control systems is to identify the functions which fit into these three blocks. For example, an electronic timing device would have an input from a switch which may be pushed manually. The process is a time delay circuit which stays on for a set length of time. The output could be a light or buzzer which indicates the time period.

*At Kew Gardens a sophisticated electronic atmosphere control system is used. Sensor detect minute changes in the conditions and blinds, ventilators and sprayers are automatically turned off and on to maintain the required atmosphere.*

## Feedback and Control

Some transformation processes serve to maintain the equilibrium, or balance, of the system. Others work to improve the quantity and/or quality of the outputs.

It is therefore possible to identify the various processes going on and to analyse whether they are maintaining the balance or working to improve quantity or quality. As a result it may be found desirable or necessary to change the inputs, or to alter the process of transformation. This is known as **feedback**.

The means by which the inputs or processes are changed are called **controls**. The success of a system is judged by how well it transforms its inputs into outputs, and how well it is prevented from failing as a result of its feedback and control elements.

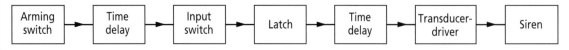

*A bike alarm*

## Production Systems

Systems are central to the management and organisation of manufacturing processes in industry and commerce. It is important that you understand how production systems work and how well they work, and are able to suggest ways in which they might be improved.

## Analysing, Evaluating and Designing Systems

Analysing a system involves identifying its structure and the changes which take place when one or more of the parts are altered.

Evaluating a system involves judging how effectively it continues to perform while the changes are taking place, and what the risks of complete failure are.

Designing a system involves creating something which will continue to operate successfully as the elements of the system change. It is also important to ensure that failure of the system will not have unacceptable consequences.

*The 'tracker' is a new electronic product designed to beat the car thief. As soon as a car fitted with the device is activated it starts transmitting a signal which can be picked up by specially equipped police patrols.*

## Using a Peripheral Interface Controller (PIC)

A PIC is a microchip that can be programmed to control a sequence of operations and react to input sensors. They can be used to reliably control complex systems. PICs are widely used in our daily lives, such as programming a video recorder. They are like a small computer, all in one economical small chip. The PIC's program can be erased and a new one downloaded. The program can be completed and simulated on screen before it is used.

### Using a PIC in your project

PICs are ideal for GCSE coursework projects, such as house alarm systems, complex games, automated vehicles and visual displays. There are many different PICs available. They vary by having different numbers and types of INPUT and OUTPUT pins. However, one of the most a useful is the 16F84 (see page 118). This has eight output and five input pins and could be used in a variety of projects.

> **KEY POINTS**
>
> - A PIC can be used to control a variety of OUTPUTs.
> - A PIC can react to an INPUT signal.
> - The program can be simulated and modified before it is downloaded to the PIC.
> - The PIC can be erased if you want to change your programme.
> - If you use a PIC decide what each of the input and output pins will do before you start.

# Choosing and Starting Projects

*Identifying suitable design and make projects for yourself is not easy. A carefully chosen project is much more likely to be interesting and easier to complete successfully. Investing time and effort in choosing a good project makes progress a lot easier later on.*

## Project Feasibility Studies

Make a start by making a list of:

▷ potential local situations/environments you could visit where you could do some research into the sort of things people there might need (e.g. a local playgroup, a small business, a hospital or sports centre, etc.)

▷ people you know outside school who might be able to help by providing information, access and/or advice.

The next stage is to get up and get going. Arrange to visit some of the situations you've listed. Choose the ones which you would be interested in finding out some more about. Make contact with the people you know, and get them interested in helping you. Tell them about your D&T course, and your project.

For each possible situation you should:

▷ visit the situation or environment
▷ make initial contact with those whose help you will need.

With a bit of luck, after you've done the above you should have a number of ideas for possible projects.

Try to identify what the possible outcomes of your projects might be – not what the final design would be, but the form your final realisation might take, e.g. a working object, a scale model, a series of plans and elevations, etc. Think carefully about the following:

▷ Might it be expensive or difficult to make?
▷ Do you have access to the tools and materials which would be required?
▷ Will you be able to find out how it could be manufactured?
▷ Does the success of the project depend on important information you might not be able to get in the time available?
▷ Are there good opportunities for you to use ICT?

the home

energy

the natural environment

the high street

transport

communications

clothing

leisure

security

food

health

education

## starting points

There are a number of different ways in which you might start a project. Your teacher may have:

● told you exactly what you are required to design
● given you a range of possible design tasks for you to choose from
● left it up to you to suggest a possible project.

If you have been given a specific task to complete you can go straight on to page 18.

If you are about to follow one of the main units in this book, you should go straight to the first page of the task.

If you have been given a number of possible tasks to choose from you should go straight to the section on page 17 entitled 'Making your Choice'.

However, if you need to begin by making some decisions about which will be best task for you, then the first stage is to undertake some project feasibility studies as described on this page.

## Making Your Choice

For each of your possible projects work through pages 18–19 (Project Investigation) and try planning out a programme of research.

Look back over your starting questions and sources of information:

▷ Could you only think up one or two areas for further research?

▷ Did you find it difficult identifying a range of sources of information?

If this has been the case, then maybe it is not going to prove to be a very worthwhile project.

Ideally, what you're looking for is a project which:

▷ is for a nearby situation you can easily use for research and testing

▷ you can get some good expert advice about.

▷ shows a good use of ICT.

It is also important that your expected outcome:

▷ will make it possible for you to make and test a prototype

▷ will not be too difficult to finally realise.

Finally, one of the most important things is that you feel interested and enthusiastic about the project!

don't forget...

A very important consideration is the testing of a prototype of some sort, and of your final design. How would you be able to do this? Could ICT be used?

Remember it's important that what you design is suitable for production, even if only in small numbers. It can't be just a one-off item. You will need to show some plans for your product to be factory made.

Don't forget to record all your thoughts and ideas about these initial stages of choosing and starting your project.

In your project folio provide a full record of the ideas you reject, and the reasons why. This helps provide important evidence of your decision-making skills, and of the originality of your project. Communication skills are important.

If you come up with more than one good idea, find out how many projects you have to submit at the end of your course. You might be able to do one or more of your other ideas at a later date.

Make sure you discuss your project ideas with a teacher.

## in my design folder

✓ My project is to design a...
✓ I am particularly interested in...
✓ I have made a very good contact with...
✓ My prototype can be tested by...
✓ My final outcome will include...
✓ I could use ICT to...

# Project Investigation

*You will need to find out as much as you can about the people and the situation you are designing for. To do this you will need to identify a number of different sources of information to use for your research.*

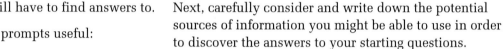

## Starting Questions

Make a list of questions you will have to find answers to.

You should find the following prompts useful:

Why...?

When...?

Where...?

What...?

How many...?

How often...?

How much...?

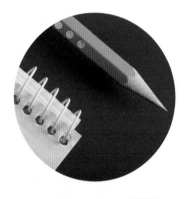

## Sources of Information

Next, carefully consider and write down the potential sources of information you might be able to use in order to discover the answers to your starting questions.

Work through the research methods on the next page. Be sure to give specific answers as far as possible (i.e. name names).

Across your research you will need to aim to obtain overall a mixture of:

▷ factual information: e.g. size, shape, weight, cost, speed, etc.
▷ information which will be a matter of opinion: i.e. what people think and feel about things, their likes and dislikes, what they find important, pleasing, frustrating, etc.

## don't forget...

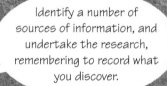

Write down what you need to find out more about, and how you could obtain the information.

Make sure your research work is clearly and attractively presented.

Identify a number of sources of information, and undertake the research, remembering to record what you discover.

You need to identify a number of sources of information (e.g. user research, existing solutions, expert opinion, information search). The wider range of methods you use, the more marks you will get.

## in my design folder

✓ The key things I need to find out about are...
✓ The research methods I am going to use are...
✓ I will be talking to the following people about my project...
✓ I will need to have it all completed by...
✓ I will use ICT to...

# Research Methods

## User Research

Which people could you observe and consult who are directly involved in the situation? To what extent do you consider that you will be able to find out about:

- the things they do
- the way in which they do them.

As well as asking individuals, you could also undertake a small survey or questionnaire.

## User Trips

How can you record your own impressions of the situation? Are there any relevant activities you could try out for yourself to gain first-hand experience? Do you have any recollections of any previous similar experiences you have had?

## Site Study

In what ways could you document the environment in which the problem is? Which of the following will be relevant?

- Historical and geographical factors.
- Sociological, economic, political information.
- Location.
- Layout, facilities.
- Sizes and spaces.
- Atmosphere – light, colour, texture.
- The surrounding environment.

## Similar Situations

Do you know of any other comparative circumstances in which people are in similar situations, and which might help provide insight and ideas?

## Expert Opinion

Are there any people you know of who could give you expert professional advice on any aspects of the situation? If you don't know immediately of anyone, how might you set about finding somebody?

## Information Search

Has any information about the situation, or a similar situation, been documented already in books, magazines, TV programmes, the Internet, or CD-ROM? If you don't already know that such information exists, where could you go to look for it? Don't forget to consider the possibility of using information stored on a computer database.

## In Conclusion

When most of your investigation work has been completed you will need to draw a series of conclusions from what you have discovered. What have you learnt about the following things:

▷ What sort of people are likely to be using the product?
▷ Where and when will they be using it?
▷ What particular features will it need to have?
▷ How many should be made?

> Of all the research methods, user-research tends to be the most effective and useful, so you are highly recommended to include some in your investigation. Some form of personal contact is essential to a really successful project.

> It is also highly advisable to conduct some form of questionnaire. If you have not done one to submit as part of your coursework, make sure that you will have the opportunity to do so this time.

> It isn't necessary to use all the research methods in any one project, but you certainly must show that you have tried a selection of them.

## in my design folder

✓ From my research I found out...
✓ I have discovered that...
✓ My conclusions are...
✓ I have kept my research relevant by...
✓ I found ICT helpful when...

# From Design Specification to Product Specification

*A design specification is a series of statements that describe the possibilities and restrictions of the product. A product specification includes details about the features and appearance of the final design, together with its materials, components and manufacturing processes.*

**ICT**

Use a word processor to draft and finalise your design specification.

## Writing a Design Specification

The **design specification** is a very important document. It describes the things about the design which are fixed and also defines the things which you are free to change.

The conclusions from your research should form the basis of your design specification. For example, if in your conclusions you wrote:

*'From the measurements I made of the distance at which a number of people could see a seven-segment display, I discovered most could read a standard display from 3 m.'*

In the specification you would simply write:

*'The display should be able to be read from 3 m.'*

The contents of the specification will vary according to the particular product you are designing, but on the next page is a checklist of aspects to consider. Don't be surprised if the specification is quite lengthy. It could easily contain 20 or more statements.

### Fixing It
Some statements in the specification will be very specific, e.g.: *'The toy must be red.'*

Other statements may be very open ended, e.g.: *'The toy can be any shape or size.'*

Most will come somewhere in between, e.g.: *'The toy should be based on a vehicle of some sort and be electronically powered.'*

In this way the statements make it clear what is already fixed (e.g. the colour), and what development is required through experimentation, testing, and modification (e.g. shape, size, vehicle-type and method of propulsion).

## Writing a Product Specification

After you have fully developed your product you will need to write a final more detailed **product specification**. This time the precise statements about the materials, components and manufacturing processes will help ensure that the manufacturer is able to make a repeatable, consistent product.

Your final product will need to be evaluated against your design specification to see how closely you have been able to meet its requirements, and against your product specification to see if you have made it correctly.

## don't forget...

You might find it helpful to start to rough out the design specification first, and then tackle the conclusions to your research. Working backwards, a sentence in your conclusion might need to read:

*'From my survey, I discovered that young children are particularly attracted by bright primary colours.'*

It's a good idea to use a word processor to write the specification. After you've written the design specification new information may come to light. If it will improve the final product, you can always change any of the statements.

Make sure you include as much numerical data as possible in your design specification. Try to provide data for anything which can be measured, such as size, weight, quantity, time and temperature.

## Specification Checklist

The following checklist is for general guidance. Not all topics will apply to your project. You may need to explore some of these topics further during your product development.

### Use and performance
Write down the main purpose of the product – what it is intended to do. Also define any other particular requirements, such as speed of operation, special features, accessories, etc. Ergonomic information is important here.

### Size and weight
The minimum and maximum size and weight will be influenced by things such as the components needed and the situation the product will be used and kept in.

Generally the smaller and lighter something is the less material it will use, reducing the production costs. Smaller items can be more difficult to make, however, increasing the production costs.

### Appearance
What shapes, colours and textures will be most suitable for the type of person who is likely to use the product? Remember that different people like different things.

These decisions will have an important influence on the materials and manufacturing processes, and are also crucial to ensure final sales.

### Safety
A product needs to conform to all the relevant safety standards.
● Which of them will apply to your design?
● How might the product be mis-used in a potentially dangerous way?
● What warning instructions and labels need to be provided?

Conforming to the regulations can increase production costs significantly, but is an area that cannot be compromised.

### Manufacturing cost
This is concerned with establishing the maximum total manufacturing cost which will allow the product to be sold at a price the consumer or client is likely to pay.

The specification needs to include details of:
● the total number of units likely to be made
● the rate of production and, if appropriate
● the size of batches.

### Maintenance
Products which are virtually maintenance free are more expensive to produce.
● How frequently will different parts of the product need to be maintained?
● How easy does this need to be?

### Life expectancy
The durability of the product has a great influence on the quantity of materials and components and the manufacturing process which will need to be used.

How long should the product remain in working order, providing it is used with reasonable care?

### Environmental requirements
In your specification you will need to take into account how your product can be made in the most environmentally friendly way. You might decide to:
● specify maximum amounts of some materials
● avoid a particular material because it can't be easily recycled
● state the use of a specific manufacturing process because it consumes less energy.

### Other areas
Other statements you might need to make might cover special requirements such as transportation and packaging.

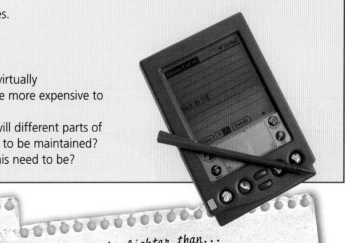

## in my design folder

✓ My design will need to...
✓ The requirements of the people who will use it are...
✓ It will also need to do the following...
✓ It will be no larger than...
✓ It will be no smaller than...
✓ Its maximum weight can be...

✓ It should not be lighter than...
✓ The shapes, colours and textures should...
✓ The design will need to conform to the following safety requirements...
✓ The number to be made is...
✓ The following parts of the product should be easily replaceable...
✓ To reduce wastage and pollution it will be necessary to ensure that...

# Generating and Developing Ideas (1)

*When you start designing you need lots of ideas – as many as possible, however crazy they might seem. Then you need to start to narrow things down a bit by working in more detail and evaluating what you are doing.*

## First Thoughts

Start by exploring possibilities at a very general level. Spend time doing some of the following:

▷ Brainstorming, using key words and phrases or questions which relate to the problem.

▷ Completing spider-diagrams which map out a series of ideas.

▷ Using random word or object-association to spark off new directions.

▷ Thinking up some good analogies to the situation (i.e. what is it like?).

▷ Work from an existing solution by changing some of the elements.

▷ Experimenting with some materials.

Continue doing this until you have at least two or three possible approaches to consider. Make sure they are all completely different, and not just a variation on one idea.

Go back to your design specification. Which of your approaches are closest to the statements you made? Make a decision about which idea to take further, and write down the reasons for your choice.

ICT ➔

Wherever possible consider using a computer to experiment with your ideas, and to analyse and present your findings.

As you work through this section it is important to remember the following sequence when considering potential solutions:

● record a number of different possibilities
● consider and evaluate each idea
● select one approach as the best course of action, stating why.

There are lots of different drawing techniques which you can use to help you explore and develop your ideas, such as plans, elevations, sections, axonometrics, perspectives, etc.
Try to use as rich a mixture of them as possible. At this stage they should really be 'rough', rather than 'formal' (i.e. drawn with a ruler). Colour is most useful for highlighting interesting ideas.

don't forget...

As usual, it is essential to record all your ideas and thoughts.

Much of your work, particularly early on, will be in the form of notes. These need to be neat enough for the examiner to be able to read.

Drawings on their own do not reveal very well what you had in mind, or whether you thought it was a good idea or not. Words on their own suggest that you are not thinking visually enough. Aim to use both sketches and words.

## Communicating your ideas

Communicating your ideas clearly and effectively through labelled drawings will help you to:

▷ visualise the ideas that you have in your head;

▷ record your ideas and your reasons for developing the product the way you have;

▷ explain your ideas to others, including your teacher and the examiner.

## Sketching

The drawing technique you use needs to be quick and clear. Sketches should be freehand - rulers should not be used as they take time and can restrict your design work to straight-line shapes.

Draw in 3D or use plans and elevations. Use colour and shade only if it helps to explain your ideas, not just to decorate the drawing. Use written notes to help explain and comment on your ideas.

## Technical Drawings

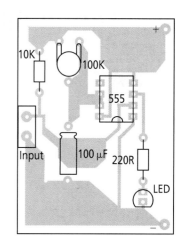

Technical drawings will help you to:

▷ produce accurate PCB masks;

▷ position components sensibly on a schematic diagram;

▷ test that the parts fit together.

For complicated details it may be necessary to draw things twice full-size (2:1), or if the product is large, half full-size (1:2). PCB masks should always be full-size (1:1).

You will need to prepare accurate technical drawings of the casing of your product before you make the final version. They should be good enough for someone else to be able to make it from.

Plans and elevations drawn together are known as **orthographic projection**. Make sure you follow the conventions for dimensioning (see page 74). Sections through the product can often help to explain constructional details, as can exploded drawings.

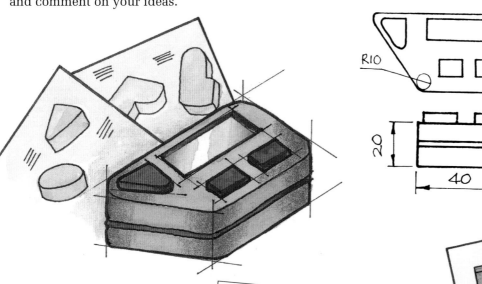

## System Diagrams

Use system and circuit diagrams to show the development of your design.

Electronic circuit diagrams should be drawn carefully using the correct symbols. PP7303 sets the standard for electrical and electronic graphical symbols.

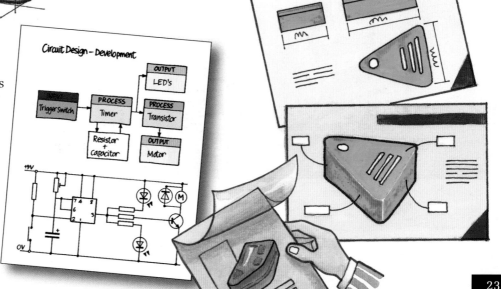

# Generating and Developing Ideas (2)

*CAD-CAM can be extremely useful at this stage. Work towards making at least one prototype to test out some specific features of your design. Record the results and continue to refine your ideas as much as you can. Sorting out the final details often requires lots of ideas too.*

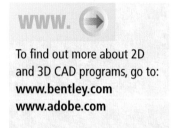

To find out more about 2D and 3D CAD programs, go to:
www.bentley.com
www.adobe.com

## CAD / CAM

**Computer Aided Design (CAD)** and **Computer Aided Manufacture (CAM)** are terms used for a range of different ICT applications that are used to help in the process of designing and making products.

**CAD** is a computer-aided system for creating, modifying and communicating ideas for a product or components of a product.

**CAM** is a broad term used when several manufacturing processes are carried out at one time aided by a computer. These may include process control, planning, monitoring and controlling production.

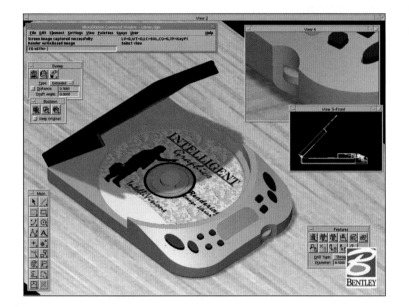

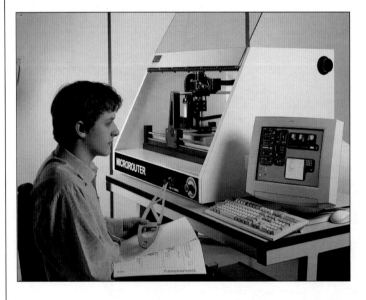

CAM or CNC systems may be used for rapid prototyping or modelling in 'soft' materials, the manufacture of small parts and moulds, and the production of templates, stencils or printouts on paper, card, vinyl, etc.

You may not have CAD-CAM or CNC systems in your workshops but you can still indicate how batch production of your product might make use of CNC machines like lathes, milling machines, flatbed routers, spindle moulders, injection and extrusion machines, etc.

## CIM

**Computer Integrated Manufacture** is extensively used by industry. This is where computers are used to control the whole production process from materials input and handling, to pick and placement, to machining to construction and possible packaging.

## ICT

Wherever possible consider using a CAD program. Designing on-screen happens very quickly and little evidence of change is seen compared with drawing on paper. You need to develop ways of recording your thinking and collect evidence of any developments.

- Make sure you print out the various stages you work through, or keep a copy on disk

- Where CAM/CNC is used you must record all your programming and evidence of machine set-ups in your project folder.

As you develop your ideas, make sure you are considering the following:
- Design – aesthetics, ergonomics, marketing potential, etc.
- User requirements – functions and features.
- Technical viability – if it could be made.
- Manufacturing potential – how it could be made in quantity.
- Environmental concerns – if it can be reused, recycled, etc.?

Models are simplified versions of intended products. Use words, numbers, drawings and 3D representations of your ideas to help you develop and evaluate your designs as they progress.

At some stage you will need to move off the drawing board and try some things out in three dimensions using real materials, circuit components and kits.

## Planning and Making Prototypes

At some stage you will be in a position to bring your ideas into sharper focus by making some form of mock-up or prototype. Think carefully about exactly what aspect of your idea you want to test out and about the sort of model which will be most appropriate.

Whatever the form of your final outcome, the prototype might need to be:

▷ two-dimensional
▷ three-dimensional
▷ made using a prototype board or system kit
▷ made using different materials at a different scale.

Try to devise some objective tests to carry out on your prototype involving measuring something. Don't rely just on people's opinions. Write up the circumstances in which the tests were undertaken, and record your results.

Write down some clear statements about:

▷ what you wanted the prototype to test
▷ the experimental conditions
▷ what you discovered
▷ what decisions you took about your design as a result.

Following your first prototype you may decide to modify it in some way and test it again, or maybe make a second, improved version from scratch. Make sure you keep all the prototypes you make, and ideally take photographs of them being tested perhaps using a digital camera.

Sometimes you will need to go back to review the decisions you made earlier, and on other occasions you may need to jump ahead for a while to explore new directions or to focus down on a particular detail. Make sure you have worked at both a general and a detailed level.

## in my design folder

✓ I chose this idea because...
✓ I developed this aspect of my design by considering...
✓ To evaluate my ideas I decided to make a prototype which...
✓ The way I tested my prototype was to...
✓ What I discovered was...
✓ As a result I decided to change...
✓ I used ICT to...

# Planning the Making and the Manufacturing

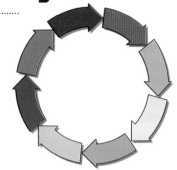

*The final realisation is very important. It presents your proposed design solution rather than the process you used to develop it. Careful planning is essential. You will also need to be able to explain how your product could be manufactured in quantity.*

### How many?

What you have designed should be suitable for manufacture. You should discuss with your teacher how many items you should attempt to make. This is likely to depend on the complexity of your design and the materials and facilities available in your workshops. It may be that you only make one item, but also provide a clear account of how a quantity of them could be manufactured.

## keeping a record

Write up a diary record of the progress you made while making. Try to include references to:
- things you did to ensure safety
- the appropriate use of materials
- minimising wastage
- choosing tools
- practising making first
- checking that what you are making is accurate enough to work
- asking experts (including teachers) for advice explaining why you had to change your original plan for making.

## A Plan of Action

Before you start planning you will need to ensure that you have an orthographic drawing of your design (see page 42). This will need to include all dimensions and details of the materials to be used.

Ideally there should also be written and drawn instructions which would enable someone else to make up the design from your plans.

Next work out a production flow chart as follows.

1  List the order in which you will make the main parts of the product. Include as much detail as you can

2  Divide the list up into a number of main stages, e.g. gathering materials and components, preparing (i.e. marking out, cutting), assembling, finishing.

3  Identify series of operations which might be done in parallel.

4  Indicate the time scale involved on an hourly, daily and weekly basis.

Consider the use of templates and jigs to help speed things up. Other possibilities include the use of moulds or setting up a simple CAM system to produce identical components.

You may find you have to change your plans as you go. There is nothing wrong with doing this, but you should explain why you have had to adjust your schedule, and show that you have considered the likely effect of the later stages of production.

Try using the Just In Time technique described on page 141.

## Quality Counts

As your making proceeds you will need to check frequently that your work is of acceptable quality. How accurately will you need to work? What tolerances will be acceptable (see page 136)? How can you judge the quality of the finish?

If you are making a number of identical items you should try and work out ways of checking the quality through a sampling process (see page 136).

## Making

While you are in the process of making you must ensure that the tools and materials you are using are the correct ones. Pay particular attention to safety instructions and guidelines.

Try to ensure that you have a finished item at the end, even if it involves simplifying what you do.

Aim to produce something which is made and finished as accurately as possible. If necessary you may need to develop and practise certain skills beforehand.

## Planning for Manufacture

Try to explain how your product would be manufactured in quantity. Work through the following stages:

1 Determine which type of production will be most suitable, depending on the number to be made.
2 Break up the production process into its major parts and identify the various sub-assemblies.
3 Consider where jigs, templates and moulding processes could be used. Where could 2D or 3D CAM be effectively used?
4 Make a list of the total number of components and volume of raw material needed for the production run.

5 Identify which parts will be made by the company and which will need to be bought in ready-made from outside suppliers.
6 Draw up a production schedule which details the manufacturing process to ensure that the materials and components will be available exactly where and when needed. How should the workforce and workspace be arranged?
7 Decide how quality control systems will be applied to

produce the degree of accuracy required.
8 Determine health and safety issues and plan to minimise risks.
9 Calculate the manufacturing cost of the product.
10 Review the design of the product and manufacturing process to see if costs can be reduced

More information on all these topics can be found on pages 120–143.

**Manufacturing matters**

Try asking the following questions about the way your design might be made in quantity:

- What work operation is being carried out, and why? What alternatives might there be?
- Where is the operation done, and why? Where else might it be carried out?
- When is it done, and why? When else might it be undertaken?
- Who carries it out, and why? Who else might do it?
- How is it undertaken, and why, How else might it be done?

Remember that manufacturing is not just about making things. It is also about making them better by making them:
- simpler  • quicker
- cheaper  • more efficient
- less damaging to the environment.

Remember to use a wide range of graphic techniques to help plan and explain your making.

Don't forget that there is also a high proportion of marks for demonstrating skill and accuracy, overcoming difficulties and working safely during the making.

What needs to be done by:
- next month
- next week
- next lesson
- the end of this lesson?

## in my design folder

✓ I planned the following sequence of making...
✓ I had to change my plan to account for...
✓ I used the following equipment and processes...
✓ I paid particular attention to safety by...
✓ I monitored the quality of my product by...
✓ My product would be manufactured in the following way...

# Testing and Evaluation

*You will need to find out how successful your final design solution is. How well does it match the design specification? How well have you worked? What would you do differently if you had another chance?*

As you work through your project you will regularly carry out testing and evaluation. For example:

▷ analysing and evaluating the research material you collected
▷ evaluating and testing carried out or existing products
▷ evaluating initial sketch ideas or prototypes and models in order to make the right decisions about which to develop further
▷ assessing the quality of your making as you go along.

Last of all, you must test hard and evaluate your final solution.

## Testing the Final Solution

To find out how successful your design is you will need to test it out. Some of the ways in which you might do this are by:

▷ trying it out yourself
▷ asking other people to use it
▷ asking experts what they think about it.

As well as recording people's thoughts, observations and opinions, try to obtain some data: how many times it worked, over what periods of time, within what performance limits, etc?

To help you decide what to test, you should look back to the statements in your design specification and focus on the most important ones. If for example the specification stated that a three-year-old child must be able to operate it, try and find out if they can. If it must be a colour which would appeal to young children, devise a way of finding out what age ranges it does appeal to.

You need to provide evidence to show that you have tested your final design out in some way. Try to ensure that your findings relate directly to the statements in your original specification. Include as much information and detail as you can.

*What methods could you use to test the success of the design of an alarm system?*

don't forget...

*Don't be too surprised or worried if your design isn't perfect – the important thing is that you can identify what needs improving. Can you make some simple suggestions about how it might be improved?*

# Final Evaluation

There are two things you need to discuss in the final evaluation: the quality of the product you have designed, and the process you went through while designing it.

## The product

How successful is your final design? Comment on things like:

▷ how it compares with your original intentions as stated in your design specification
▷ how well it solves the original problem
▷ the materials you used
▷ what it looks like
▷ how well it works
▷ what a potential user said
▷ what experts said
▷ whether it could be manufactured cheaply enough in quantity to make a profit
▷ the effective use of ICT to assist reproduction or manufacture
▷ the extent to which it meets the requirements of the client, manufacturer and the retailer
▷ the ways in which it could be improved.

Justify your evaluation by including references to what happened when you tested it.

## The process

How well have you worked? Imagine you suddenly had more time, or were able to start again, and consider:

▷ Which aspects of your investigation, design development work and making would you try to improve, or approach in a different way?
▷ What did you leave to the last minute, or spend too much time on?
▷ Which parts are you most pleased with, and why?
▷ How well did you make the final realisation?
▷ How effective was your use of ICT? How did it enhance your work?

If you had more time:
● what aspects of the product would you try to improve? (refer to your evaluation if you can).
● how would you improve the way you had researched, developed, planned and evaluated your working process?

## in my design folder

What do you think you have learnt through doing the project?
✓ Comparison of my final product specification with my design specification showed that...
✓ The people I showed my ideas (drawings and final product) to said...
✓ I was able to try my design out by...
✓ I discovered that...
✓ I could improve it by...
✓ I didn't do enough research into...
✓ I spent too long on...
✓ I should have spent more time on...
✓ The best aspect is...
✓ I have learnt a lot about...

Try to identify a mixture of good and bad points about your final proposal and method of working. You will gain credit for being able to demonstrate that you are aware of weaknesses in what you have designed and the way that you have designed it.

If people have been critical of aspects of your design, do you agree with them? Explain your response.

Remember that evaluation is on-going. It should also appear throughout your project whenever decisions are made. Explain the reasons behind your actions.

Don't forget to write about both the product and the process.

# Project Presentation

*The way you present your project work is extremely important. Remember you won't be there to explain it all when it's being assessed! You need to make it as easy as possible for an examiner to see and understand what you have done.*

## Telling the Story

All your investigation and development work needs to be handed in at the end, as well as what you have made. Your design folder needs to tell the story of the project. Each section should lead on from the next, and show clearly what happened next, and explain why. Section titles and individual page titles can help considerably.

There is no single way in which you must present your work, but the following suggestions are all highly recommended:

▷ Securely bind all the pages together in some way. Use staples or treasury tags. There is no need to buy an expensive folder.
▷ Add a cover with a title and an appropriate illustration.
▷ Make it clear which the main sections are.
▷ Add titles or running headings to each sheet to indicate what aspect of the design you were considering at that particular point in the project.

Remember to include evidence of ICT work and other Key Skills. Carefully check through your folder and correct any spelling and punctuation mistakes.

## Presenting your Design Project Sheets

▷ Always work on standard-size paper, either A3 or A4.

▷ Aim to have a mixture of written text and visual illustration on each sheet.

▷ You might like to design a special border to use on each sheet.

▷ Include as many different types of illustration as possible.

▷ When using photographs, use a small amount of adhesive applied evenly all the way around the edge to secure them to your folder sheet.

▷ Think carefully about the lettering for titles, and don't just put them anywhere and anyhow. Try to choose a height and width of lettering which will be well balanced on the whole page. If the title is too big or boldly coloured it may dominate the sheet. If it is thin or light it might not be noticed.

## don't forget...

Presentation is something you need to be thinking about throughout your project work.

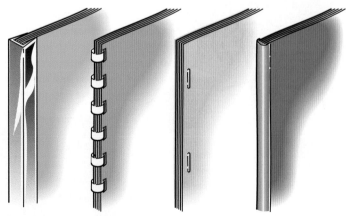

*Binding methods*

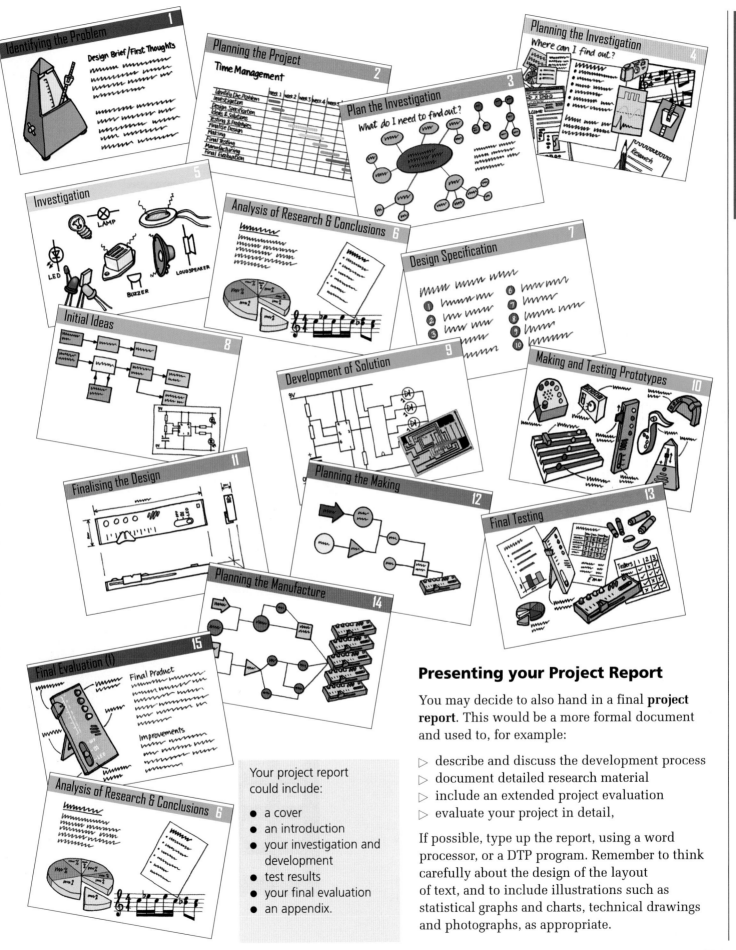

## Presenting your Project Report

You may decide to also hand in a final **project report**. This would be a more formal document and used to, for example:

▷ describe and discuss the development process
▷ document detailed research material
▷ include an extended project evaluation
▷ evaluate your project in detail,

If possible, type up the report, using a word processor, or a DTP program. Remember to think carefully about the design of the layout of text, and to include illustrations such as statistical graphs and charts, technical drawings and photographs, as appropriate.

Your project report could include:

● a cover
● an introduction
● your investigation and development
● test results
● your final evaluation
● an appendix.

# Project One: Introduction

*For centuries locks and keys have been one of the main ways of securing personal property.*

*Modern electronics has now made it possible to replace keys. Can you design and make an electronic lock which opens when the correct combination of switches is chosen from a keypad?*

Solenoids
(page 49)

ELECTRONIC SECURITY

Interface Devices
(page 46)

Prototype Boards
(page 44)

Entry to our houses, cars and personal belongings such as luggage is often controlled by keys. The detailed design of each lock and key combination needs to be unique.

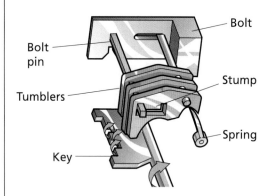

Bolt

Bolt pin

Stump

Tumblers

Spring

Key

## New Combinations

Electronics has made it possible to replace keys with security systems based on a code number which is typed into a keypad.

Electronic locks are generally found on rooms, cash dispensers, safes, filing cabinets and vehicles such as cars and lorries. Personal items such as luggage could also be fitted with electronic locks.

The advantages of electronic security systems are that:

▷ there are no keys to lose;
▷ the combination can be changed easily if necessary.

What possible disadvantages of electronic code locking systems can you think of?

A large number of digital combinations can be selected from just a few switches. If three numbers (digits) can be arranged in six unique combinations, how many different combinations will a ten-digit display offer?

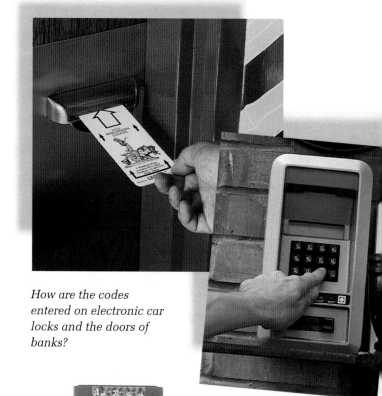

*How are the codes entered on electronic car locks and the doors of banks?*

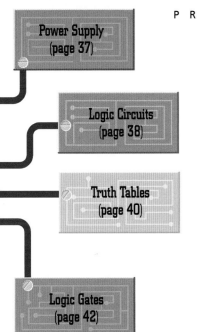

Power Supply
(page 37)

Logic Circuits
(page 38)

Truth Tables
(page 40)

Logic Gates
(page 42)

## The Task

You are asked to design and make an electronic lock and keypad for a container of some sort. Identify some specific items which your lock will be suitable for. It might be something you use at home or at school.

Write a brief description of the container and where and how an electronic lock could be attached.

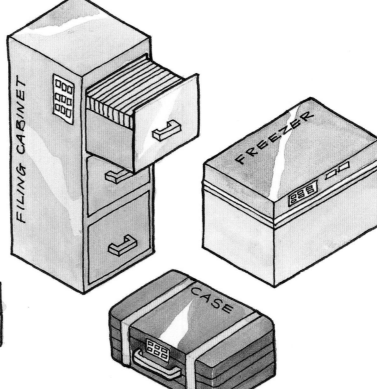

## ■ ACTIVITY

Investigate some of the common uses for electronic locks and switches. Sketch examples you find, and write brief accounts which include how the locks are contained.

The container I am going to design a lock for is.....

The lock must only open when the code is typed in correctly. Any other variation must not work.

If someone enters the wrong code......

# Product Analysis

*Before designers start to develop new ideas, they need to understand how existing products work and how people use them. They also look closely at the materials which have been used, and how they have been manufactured.*

## Investigate, Disassemble and Evaluate

You need to understand the general principles of how a product works before you can begin to design. Write a brief description of the electronic door lock illustrated on the right. Try to explain how it works.

The keypad provides a code which releases the...

## Existing Solutions

It is always useful to look closely at a range of products which have the same function as the product you are about to design.

From an initial investigation you should be able to describe some of the important features. Try asking yourself questions like:

▷ What should it do? Does it?
▷ What shouldn't it do? Does it?
▷ What is the most important thing it should do?
▷ How might it do this better?

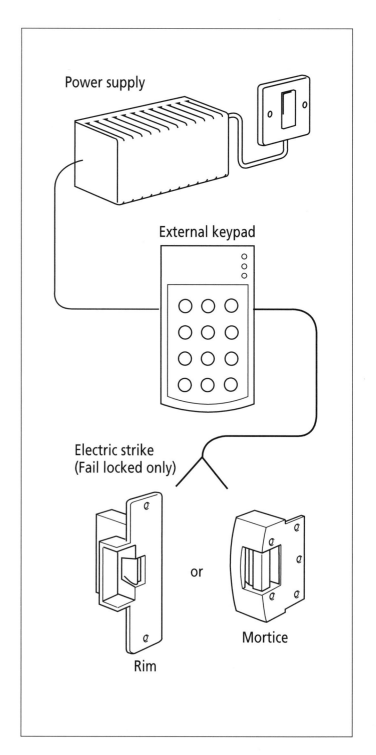

Power supply

External keypad

Electric strike
(Fail locked only)

Rim      or      Mortice

## Getting Down to Detail

The next step is to focus on the component parts that make up the product. For example:

▷ What does the whole product do?
▷ What does the part look like?
▷ What does the part do?
▷ Does it move, make a sound, flash, etc?
▷ What makes it do these things?
▷ What is it made from?
▷ How was it manufactured?

Record your observations and thoughts with sketches as well as words.

## Sources of Information

Advertising material from manufacturers is a useful way of finding out what they think customers want.

## Open Locks

Examine a variety of locking devices. Focus on the bolt.

▷ What shape is it?
▷ What length is it?
▷ How tightly does it fit?
▷ How is it secured?

## Security Survey

Interview some people you know about when, how and why they use keys at home and at work. Choose a variety of people from different occupations.

Before you meet them, devise a brief questionnaire. Be careful not to ask them things which they might not want to tell you about. Reassure them that you will not record their name or address.

Record their answers and display them as a pie chart. A computer spreadsheet system will produce excellent graphs for your design folio.

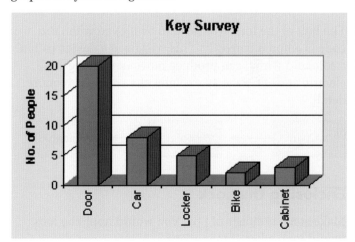

## Data Protection

You could use a digital camera to make a record of your interview. You could also use a spreadsheet or databases to record the information people give you. If you do you need to be aware of the Data Protection Act. This act applies to the electronic collection, storage and distribution of personal data about living individuals. Among other things, the act requires data to be accurate, only used for lawful purposes, and to be held securely. It also states that an individual must have access to the data so it can be checked for accuracy.

### QUESTIONNAIRE

Age Range .......................................... M/F
Occupation ...............................................

How many keys do you carry round with you? .........

What are they used for?...............................
.........................................................
.........................................................

What other keys do you use:

At home? ...............................................

At work? ...............................................

Do you think electronic locks are more secure than traditional locks?     Yes/No

# First Thoughts

*Before getting down to some detailed experiments with electronic components you will need to think carefully about the main elements of the system.*

To find out more about batteries, go to:
**www.duracell.com**

## Logic

Designing a digital lock calls for a series of 'logical decisions', e.g:

▷ *If the code is correct then open the lock*, or
▷ *If the code is incorrect then sound an alarm.*

Electronic systems which are designed to make decisions are called **logic circuits** and are made up of **logic gates**. Page 38 contains a guide to logic circuits.

## Solenoid

The bolt of the lock will need to be moved when the code is entered correctly. This will need a device called a solenoid which can produce movement using an electric current. Page 49 explains the solenoid in more detail.

Keypad → Logic → Solenoid

## Enclosing the Lock

Make some sketches of how you would hope the lock would look when it is in place.

▷ Will the keypad be flush with the surface or raised in some sort of container?

If you are planning to add the lock to an existing product it will need a very robust container.

▷ How will the solenoid need to be secured and contained?

## The Power Supply

▷ What power supply would be most suitable?
▷ If a battery is used, what type will it be?
▷ How long is it likely to last?
▷ Will the lock open when the battery discharges?
▷ How will you make changing the battery easy?

## Choosing a Power Supply

| Battery or cell | Size & shape | Cost | Advantages & limitations | Voltage | Common uses |
|---|---|---|---|---|---|
| Solar cells | 45 x 26 mm up to 310 x 160 mm | 62p – £16 | Performance depends on the amount of light | 0.45 – 12 V | Power source for low-current circuits, powering low-inertia motors, battery charging |
| Zinc–carbon | AAA<br>AA<br>C<br>D<br>PP3 | 23p<br>23p<br>41p<br>45p<br>90p | Can leak after a time. Voltage drops if too large a current is drawn | 1.5 V | Torches, radios, toys |
| Zinc–carbon (sealed) e.g. Silver seal | AAA<br>AA<br>C<br>D<br>PP3 | 69p<br>69p<br>£1.27<br>£1.38<br>£2.36 | Less likely to leak and deliver more current when used continuously | 1.5 V<br>1.5 V<br>1.5 V<br>1.5 V<br>9 V | Portable cassette players, calculators |
| Alkaline/ manganese cells | AAA<br>AA<br>C<br>D<br>PP3 | £1.05<br>50p<br>£1.50<br>£1.50<br>£2.50 | High performance with corrosion-free construction | 1.5 V<br>1.5 V<br>1.5 V<br>1.5 V<br>9.0 V | Circuits with a high current drain such as motors (e.g. toys), cassette players, general circuit board work |
| NiCad cells | AAA<br>AA<br>C<br>D<br>PP3 | £2.25<br>£3.37<br>£3.13<br>£5.61<br>£4.54 | Rechargeable 100s of times. (Remember a charger unit is needed) | 1.2 V<br>1.2 V<br>1.2 V<br>1.2 V<br>8.4 V | Motorised toys, cassette recorders, general circuit board work |
| Mercury button cells | Button | 50p – £1.50 | miniature | 1.35 – 1.4 V | Calculators, watches |
| Silver oxide button cells | Button | 50 – 99p | miniature | 1.4 V | Calculator watches, musical outputs |
| Lead–acid batteries | 70 x 47 x 109 mm to car battery size | | Rechargeable, high current, large capacity | 6 V or 12 V | Tools, wheelchairs, car alarms |
| Mains power supplies (transformed) | Universal d.c. power supply | £2 – £5 | Not portable but cheap power for non-mobile applications | 3 – 12 V | Cassette players, most circuit board work, domestic alarms |

A series of cells stacked together is called a **battery**. Most voltages above 1.5 V are produced by putting a number of cells together in series (even if they look like a single cell).

How many 1.5 V zinc–carbon cells are stacked inside a PP3 battery?

**IN YOUR PROJECT**

Identify a suitable power supply. Describe it in terms of its size, price, and its advantages and disadvantages.

# Logic Circuits

*Logic circuits can make simple decisions. In the same way as a garden gate opens and closes, electronic logic gates can be said to open or close, switching things on and off.*

There are a variety of circuits that have names to indicate the logical decision they make when their inputs are connected to a power supply.

## Mechanical Logic Circuits

Logical decisions can be made using mechanical switches. If two switches are connected in series as part of an electrical circuit, the output motor will only start when switch A and switch B are closed.

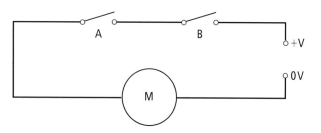

This circuit is a simple example of an AND gate circuit. These are commonly used as a safety device in electrical machinery such as washing machines and microwave cookers.

### ■ ACTIVITY

Explain how the AND safety circuit works to protect the user if the door on a microwave is not closed correctly.

### ■ ACTIVITY

On the right is an example of an OR gate. What possible uses can you think of for this type of system?

## Electronic Logic Gates

Electronic logic gates are components whose main use is in multi-input devices to 'decide' when certain things have happened. They can also be used to make other electronic circuits such as monostables, bistables and astables.

Logic gates have two or more inputs and one output. The symbol for a 2-input AND gate is shown on page 39 opposite.

The function of each logic gate is described by its truth table (see page 40).

In a circuit made by connecting two switches in parallel, one or the other, or both of them, could be used to switch on a device. This is a simple OR circuit.

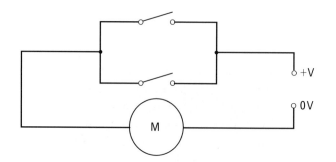

> Logic gates are digital devices. This means they do not have any in-between states, such as half-on or half-off.

## Integrated Circuits

Designers of electronic products use logic gates as components in the form of **integrated circuits** or ICs. An integrated circuit is a tiny piece of semi-conducting material into which a very complex circuit is cut. Because the semi-conducting material is made of silicon, ICs are often called silicon chips or 'chips' for short.

ICs behave as though they are composed of many different electronic components, such as transistors, resistors and capacitors. An IC such as the 4001 may contain the equivalent of 30 or 40 individual electronic components.

Microelectronics technology has developed the ability to place millions of components together within just a few square millimetres on an IC. Most of the bulk of the component is a casing in which leads run to the connection pins of the IC. These enable it to be connected into a circuit.

The 4081 IC shown on the right is a quad 2-input AND gate IC. This means it has four separate AND gates, each of which has two inputs. They are packaged in a rectangle of plastic with legs, or pins, arranged in pairs down the side. This is often referred to as dual-in-line or DIL for short.

*The IC itself is very small*

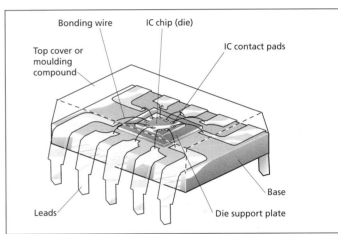

## CMOS Logic Gate ICs

Most of the logic gate ICs mentioned in this book belong to the CMOS family of chips. They are cheap, reasonably robust and work well with a range of supply voltages (3–15 V). Connections are made through the 14 pins.

These pins are numbered and you need to refer to the pin layout when connecting up the logic gates. The pin layouts for two ICs are shown opposite. There is a spot or a notch at one end of the case to help you locate pin 1.

If you use these chips in your circuits, make sure you connect any unused inputs to either the +V or 0V rail. Unused outputs should be left unconnected. Don't forget to 'power up' the IC itself by connecting pin 14 to +V and pin 7 to 0 V. Try not to touch the pins with your fingers since the chips are slightly sensitive to static.

**OR gate**

A
B — Q

**AND gate**

A
B — Q

> Symbols are used because they make circuits easier to draw, and usually take up less space than the component they represent.
>
> You may be familiar with some of them already, but eventually you will need to be able to recognise all of those shown on page 61.

> You will need to use diagrams like those below to help you make the right connections as you experiment with your circuits.

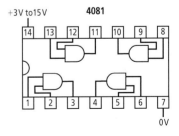

### ■ ACTIVITY

Identify the AND gate IC and the OR gate IC on the diagrams above.

# Truth Tables

*Truth tables are used to show the outputs of logic circuits for all of the possible combinations of inputs.*

*The tables are useful for helping to design decision-making circuits and to decide whether an idea is likely to work as you expect.*

When describing the action of logic gates, their inputs and outputs are commonly represented as:

▷ logic '0' for 'off' or 'low';
▷ logic '1' for 'on' or 'high'.

## AND and OR Truth Tables

A truth table uses the symbols 0 and 1 to represent all the possible inputs and outputs.

If you look at the truth table for an AND gate you can see that the gate is expected to only give a 'high' output at Q if both inputs A and B are 'high'.

Look at the truth table for the OR gate. Can you explain what combinations of inputs at A and B give 'high' outputs?

Which one of these two logic circuits would be most useful if you were designing a combination lock in which the output at Q opened the lock?

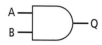

| A | B | Q |
|---|---|---|
| 0 | 0 | 0 |
| 0 | 1 | 0 |
| 1 | 0 | 0 |
| 1 | 1 | 1 |

*AND gate*

| A | B | Q |
|---|---|---|
| 0 | 0 | 0 |
| 0 | 1 | 1 |
| 1 | 0 | 1 |
| 1 | 1 | 1 |

*OR gate*

## ■ ACTIVITY

Use AND and OR logic ICs to test whether the outputs behave as predicted by the truth tables.

You could do this by using systems kits or by making up circuits on prototype board using logic gate ICs. Page 44 shows how to use a prototype board to connect up a logic gate IC.

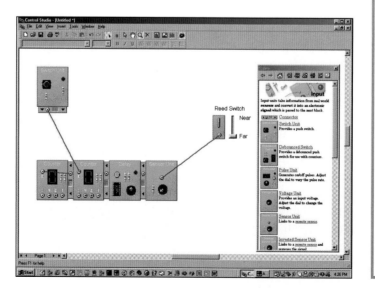

## KEY POINTS

● Logic gates are used in circuits where there are more than one input.
● Logic gate ICs are digital devices; the output is 'on' or 'off', often decribed as 'high' or 'low'.
● Using the number 1 for 'high' and 0 for 'low', truth tables can be used to describe the function of different logic gates.

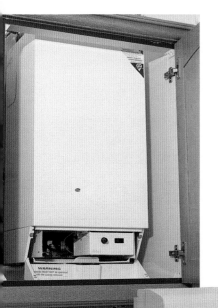

## Solving Problems with Logic Gates

Most homes have a central heating system which can maintain the temperature of the house at a steady level. Energy must be supplied if the temperature drops, and switched off when the temperature reaches the required level.

A digital logic circuit can provide this type of control. Truth tables are used to check that the correct decisions will be made by the circuitry. In a gas-fired system the gas valve must only open when there is a pilot light to ignite the main gas supply. The logic gate must have a 'high' output (logic 1) to turn on the gas valve.

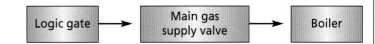

The logic gate must only go 'high' when:

1 the output from a thermostat is 'high'. This happens when a sensor detects that the temperature is too low. Generally, this temperature is set by a room thermostat; *and*

2 the output from a pilot flame sensor is 'high', indicating that the pilot light is on.

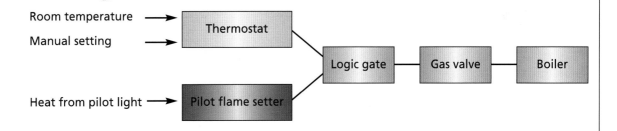

### ■ ACTIVITY

Examine the truth tables on the right.
▶ Which one would be a suitable logic gate to include in the central heating system?
▶ What type of sensor would be useful in a thermostat?
▶ How could the heat from a pilot light flame be used to close a connection in order to provide a 'high' output?

| A | B | Q |
|---|---|---|
| 0 | 0 | 0 |
| 0 | 1 | 0 |
| 1 | 0 | 0 |
| 1 | 1 | 1 |

| A | B | Q |
|---|---|---|
| 0 | 0 | 0 |
| 0 | 1 | 1 |
| 1 | 0 | 1 |
| 1 | 1 | 1 |

# Logic Gates

*The output from one logic gate can be fed into the input of another gate to produce a logic gate with different characteristics. Gates of this sort have such useful functions that they have their own symbols and are produced as integrated circuits.*

+3V to15V     **4069**

| A | Q |
|---|---|
| 0 | 1 |
| 1 | 0 |

## NOT Gates

NOT gates give a 'high' output when supplied with a 'low' input and a 'low' output with a 'high' input. They are also called **inverters** and have only one input.

## NAND Gates

The outputs of a NAND gate are the opposite of those for an AND gate. A NAND gate behaves the same as an AND gate connected in series with a NOT gate. To simplify the symbols, the NOT is added as a small circle to the gate symbol.

The truth table outputs are the opposite of those for an AND gate.

NAND

| A | B | Q |
|---|---|---|
| 0 | 0 | 1 |
| 0 | 1 | 1 |
| 1 | 0 | 1 |
| 1 | 1 | 0 |

NOR

| A | B | Q |
|---|---|---|
| 0 | 0 | 1 |
| 0 | 1 | 0 |
| 1 | 0 | 0 |
| 1 | 1 | 0 |

## NOR Gates

The outputs for a NOR gate are the opposite of those for an OR gate. A NOR gate behaves the same as an OR gate connected in series with a NOT gate.

## XOR (eXclusive OR) Gate

The exclusive OR gate is a variation on an OR gate. It gives a 'high' output if either of the inputs is 'high' but 'low' if *both* inputs are 'high' or 'low'.

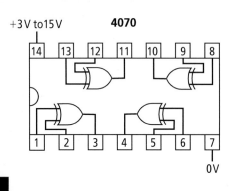

+3V to15V     **4070**

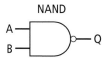

XOR

| A | B | Q |
|---|---|---|
| 0 | 0 | 0 |
| 0 | 1 | 1 |
| 1 | 0 | 1 |
| 1 | 1 | 0 |

■ **ACTIVITY**

Confirm the truth tables for the NOT, NOR and NAND gates using prototype boards or systems kits. You will need to be familiar with wiring these chips as you begin to design circuits for your projects.

■ **ACTIVITY**

An XOR gate could be used as part of a circuit to help 'referee' quiz games. Describe how it would work using a 4070 IC.

| Symbol | Description | Truth table | | | IC pin configuration |
|--------|-------------|-------------|---|---|---------------------|
| **AND**<br>A ⊐ Q<br>B | Gives a 'high' output only when both inputs are 'high'. | A B Q | | | +3V to15V   **4081** |

**AND** truth table:

| A | B | Q |
|---|---|---|
| 0 | 0 | 0 |
| 0 | 1 | 0 |
| 1 | 0 | 0 |
| 1 | 1 | 1 |

**OR** — Output 'high' unless both inputs are 'low'.

| A | B | Q |
|---|---|---|
| 0 | 0 | 0 |
| 0 | 1 | 1 |
| 1 | 0 | 1 |
| 1 | 1 | 1 |

IC: +3V to15V **4071**

**NOT** — Inverter – output always opposite of the input.

| A | Q |
|---|---|
| 0 | 1 |
| 1 | 0 |

IC: +3V to15V **4069**

## Using NAND Gates to Make Other Logic Gates

All of the logic gates shown in the table above can be made by combining NAND gates, like the ones shown here. This principle can be used to reduce the number of different ICs you might need to make a range of circuits. Why do you think this might be useful?

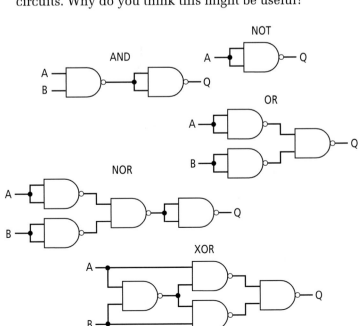

### ■ ACTIVITY

▶ Extend the table above for NOR, NAND and XOR gates.
▶ Using a prototype board or systems kit make up an XOR gate from the NAND gates in a 4011 IC.

### Investigation

Logic gate ICs can be used to make a wide variety of simple electronic products. You might wish to find out about their use in products such as timers and electronic locks. There are many useful books available which will help you in your research.

**ICT** ⊙

You could use CAD software such as Crocodile Clips to learn how logic works.

### IN YOUR PROJECT

NAND gates can be very useful in coursework projects, but will not be tested in the written examination

### KEY POINTS

● Logic gates can be used to make a wide range of electronic devices such as monostables, bistables, astables, reaction timers and electronic locks.
● AND, OR, NOR, NOT and XOR gates can all be made from NAND gates.

# Prototype Boards and Systems Kits

*As you develop your knowledge of electronic solutions to design problems you will need to start to experiment by making up a number of circuits. There are a range of systems which enable you to produce temporary circuits that do not require components to be permanently soldered together.*

## Prototype Boards

The prototype board method for producing circuits is illustrated below. These boards are sometimes called 'breadboards'.

Vertical holes are connected in columns of 5 – A to E and F to J

Integrated circuit

Supply positive lines

Horizontal holes are connected in two rows up to middle point

Chips (ICs) and transistors are usually placed across the gap

Transistor

Supply negative lines

*The legs of the components used in the prototype circuit are just pushed into the holes of the board and are connected by clips at the back of the holes*

### Practical notes

You are more likely to have success when building circuits on prototype board if you follow a few simple rules.

▶ Use the top and bottom horizontal rows of holes for the +V and 0V lines respectively (note – they are only joined as far as the middle gap).

▶ Use the vertical columns of holes (A to E and F to J) as joining points for components and wires (note – these columns act as the dots on the circuit diagram).

▶ Use insulated single-strand wire to link the columns where necessary.

▶ Work left to right and +V to 0V when building the circuit –

don't 'jump about', you'll miss out something.

▶ Don't connect the power supply until the circuit is complete.

▶ If the circuit doesn't work, check that you have built it up correctly. If you have, try swapping connection columns – the clips on the back of them wear out with use.

1K resistors     4011 integrated circuit

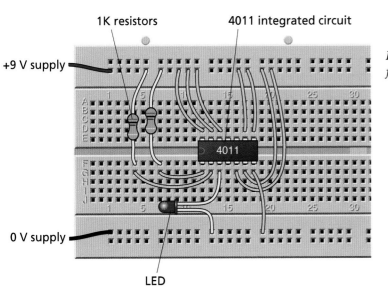

+9 V supply

*Prototype board layout
for NAND gate testing*

4011

0 V supply

LED

### IN YOUR PROJECT

If you are working with an unfamiliar circuit, or one you have designed yourself, it is sensible to test whether it works before building it on a permanent circuit board.

### ■ ACTIVITY

Build the circuit as shown and test whether the gate works as its truth table suggests.

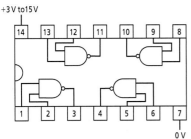

+3 V to 15 V

| 14 | 13 | 12 | 11 | 10 | 9 | 8 |

| 1 | 2 | 3 | 4 | 5 | 6 | 7 |

0 V

*Pin layout for a 4011 IC*

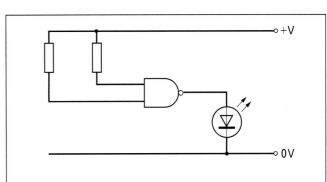

+V

0V

## Systems Kits

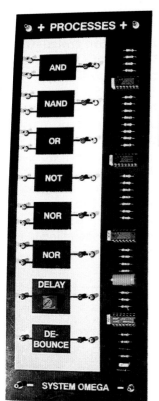

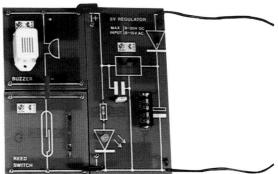

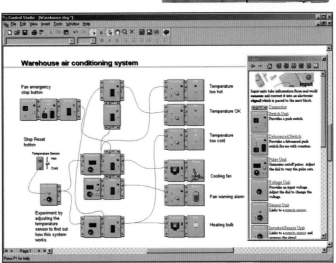

Warehouse air conditioning system

*Your school may have systems kits like the one shown here. These are very useful when investigating the function of logic gates and their truth tables because they are so simple to set up.*

*You can investigate the different functions of components by using on screen simulations or by using project board.*

# Interface Devices: Transducer-Drivers (1)

*Microelectronic devices such as logic gate ICs use only minute currents in their operation. Many output devices used in electronic circuits require a relatively large current to operate properly. Transducer-driver circuits protect the input circuit by only using a small current which switches on another circuit in which a larger current flows.*

**ICT** →

You could use a CD-ROM component catalogue to find for your required transistor

Most of the sensing and processing building block circuits described in this book only output a low-value current. They may therefore need to be linked to the output device or transducer via an interface circuit. These circuits are commonly called transducer-drivers. They can be made from relays, transistors or operational amplifiers.

## IN YOUR PROJECT

A logic gate will require a transducer-driver circuit to operate a solenoid.

## ■ ACTIVITY

Make a list of output transducers and against each one describe the energy transfer, e.g. a bulb transfers electrical energy to heat and light.

## ■ ACTIVITY

What base voltage do you think is needed to turn the Darlington pair on?

### Output transducers
The output from most electronic devices is some sort of transducer. Transducers change electrical energy into some other form of energy. Bulbs, motors, buzzers, bells, loudspeakers and solenoids are common examples.

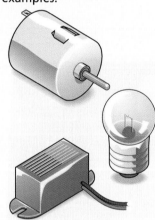

### npn transistors
The most common type of transistor you will use is an npn bipolar transistor. The transistor is controlled by the **base** connection and the output device is connected to either the **collector** or the **emitter**. The emitter is connected to 0V and the collector to +V.

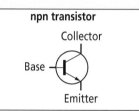

*npn transistor*

npn transistors switch on when an input of around 0.6V is supplied to the base. They are **analogue** devices and allow a larger current to flow through the collector/emitter as the base current increases. A base voltage of around 1.4V turns the transistor fully on.

### Transistor gain
Transistors are **current amplifiers**. The amplification is known as the **gain**. The gain of the transistor is calculated using the equation:

$$h_{FE} = \frac{I_c}{I_b}$$

$h_{FE}$ = gain
$I_c$ = collector current
$I_b$ = base current

### Transistor cases
It is important that you identify the base, collector and emitter correctly when you use transistors. The diagrams show some common types of case but

you should always check in the supplier's catalogue. See page 127 for more information.

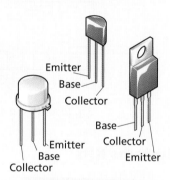

### Darlington transistors
The gain of a transistor can be increased by connecting it to a second transistor in a Darlington pair arrangement. You can buy Darlington transistors which work in the same way. A TIP120 is an example. Darlington transistors have the advantage of higher gain and power handling capacity.

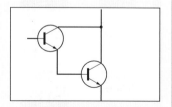

*A Darlington pair*

46

# Relays

A relay is an electromechanical device which uses a small control current to switch a much larger load current. The control circuit is isolated from the load circuit. Relays are used in switching circuits where the output of that circuit has insufficient power to drive the output device. Their main disadvantages are that they can only operate at low switching speeds and are relatively expensive.

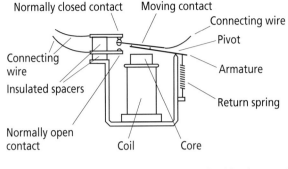

*A double throw relay*

DIL reed relay

Miniature relay

Continental relay

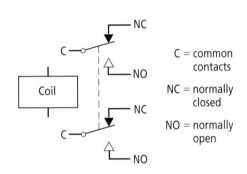

*Relay circuit symbol (shown with DPDT contacts)*

C = common contacts

NC = normally closed

NO = normally open

## Using a Relay as a Latch

If the output of a circuit needs to be kept 'high' or 'low' once it is triggered, then a latching circuit is usually required. More information about latch circuits can be found on pages 88–89.

As well as switching larger currents, a relay with double pole double throw (DPDT) contacts can be used to latch a switching circuit. The relay coil is connected between the transistor collector and +V and one set of contacts is connected to the collector and 0 V. The other set of contacts switches the output device.

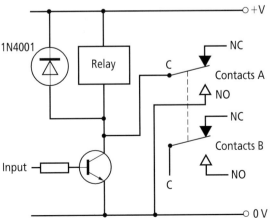

■ **ACTIVITY**

Find out what is meant by the terms:
▶ coil
▶ armature
▶ common, normally open and normally closed contacts
▶ double pole double throw.

Refer to the diagram at the top of the page to explain briefly how a relay works.

## How It Works

When the transistor is switched on by an input to the base connection, the relay coil is energised and the common contacts switch across to the normally open contacts. This makes a path for current to flow through the relay coil, via the common and normally open contacts of set A, without passing through the transistor.

The relay therefore stays on even when the transistor switches off. To turn the latch off, the relay coil must be de-energised. How do you think this could be done?

# Interface Devices: Transducer-Drivers (2)

## Field Effect Transistors (FETs)

Field effect transistors are voltage amplifiers rather than current amplifiers. They can be switched on by a very small input voltage applied to the gate. This makes them useful as amplifiers for low-powered process circuits such as CMOS logic gates.

This property also makes them a good choice for electronic switches controlled by high-resistance inputs, e.g. touch switches (see pages 68–69).

In normal use, the **drain** is connected to +V via the output device, the **source** is connected to 0 V and the **gate** to the input.

Discuss the advantages of using software such as Crocodile Clips.

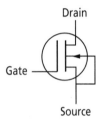

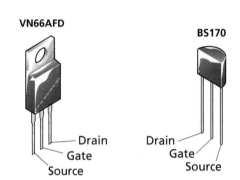

VN66AFD

BS170

Drain
Gate
Source

Drain
Gate
Source

FETs, like npn transistors, are made in a variety of forms. The types which can handle high currents usually have metal heat sinks (e.g. VN66AFD). What do you think is meant by 'heat sink'?

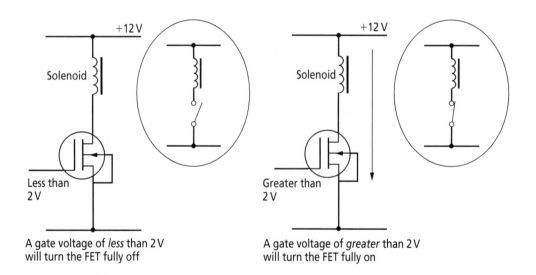

A gate voltage of *less* than 2 V will turn the FET fully off

A gate voltage of *greater* than 2 V will turn the FET fully on

### IN YOUR PROJECT

Remember that FETs can be damaged by static electricity so try not to touch the legs with your fingers.

### KEY POINTS

- Many output devices require more current than can safely be carried by logic circuits. These require a driver circuit.
- Bipolar transistors are current amplifiers and are used as transducer-drivers and electronic switches.
- npn transistors are the most common type – the gain is given by $I_c/I_b$.
- A relay uses a small control current to switch on a larger current.
- FETs are voltage amplifiers and are useful in high impedance circuits.

# Solenoids

*A solenoid is an electromagnetic device which produces linear movement when a current flows in a coil of wire.*

*Solenoid symbol*

## Operating the Lock Mechanism

A solenoid is a good choice for the output of your electronic lock circuit.

Solenoids are made up of a coil of wire surrounding a movable iron core. The iron core is attracted into the coil of wire when a current flows. When the current is switched off the spring inside the solenoid pushes the iron core out again. The current needed to operate the solenoid is more than the logic circuit can deliver without overheating. A suitable transducer-driver circuit from those shown on pages 44–47 is therefore needed.

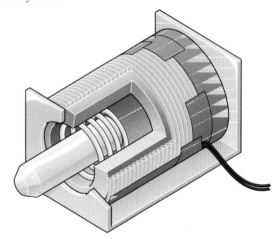

▷ What voltage does your solenoid require to operate?
▷ The circuit will need a suitable power supply. Will this be a battery? How many operations will it provide energy for?
▷ The lock needs to be reset (i.e. locked) once opened. Will this be automatic after a set period of time or will it be a manual operation?

The logic gates and transducer-driver will need to be soldered together as neatly as possible on a permanent board. How to produce permanent circuits is shown on page 51.

**IN YOUR PROJECT**

Solenoids can be very useful in coursework projects but will not be tested in the written examination.

# Developing the Lock

*Electronic building blocks such as logic gates, transducer-driver circuits and output devices need to be selected to produce the required system.*

If possible, use PCB software to develop your PCB design. Try using the AutoRoute facility as well as your own design.

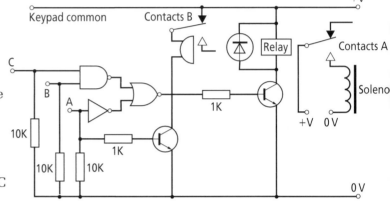

## Opening and Closing the Lock

A keypad is a series of switches which are arranged to provide inputs to the logic circuit. A 'common bus' type is the most useful.

On the right is a possible circuit which requires the correct three buttons to be pressed in sequence. If keys connected to B and C are pressed and then A, the lock opens. If keys connected to A are pressed before B and C the buzzer sounds.

Power supply → Keypad → Logic → Transducer-driver → Solenoid

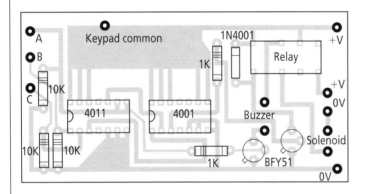

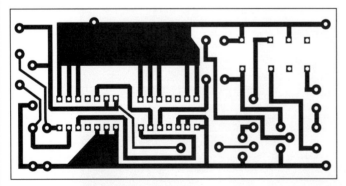

## ■ ACTIVITY

Draw the truth table for the logic gates above. Use the truth table to explain how the lock will function.

## Choosing a Code

Using more switches which are not connected means that it is harder to find the correct code. The other switches will need to set off an alarm or could also lock out further attempts to find the code.

A series of logic gates can produce a system which would set off the alarm unless the two correct buttons were pressed before any others.

A possible PCB and component layout for the alarm circuit and the lock is shown on the left.

## Developing Your Design

You may wish to develop this basic electronic solution to produce a more sophisticated design.

▷ Circuits similar to that shown above could be used to connect up the remaining keys of a pad to make it more difficult to find the right combination.
▷ A timing circuit could relock the door after a set time. Timing circuits are discussed on pages 62–63.
▷ A relay used as a latch (see page 47) would hold the bolt back until the device is reset.
▷ Would a sound as each button is pressed help the user?
▷ A more sophisticated system could sense when each switch is pressed in sequence. This will require logic gates to be connected to components called latches or bistables. See pages 86–88 for more information on bistables.

# Making Your Circuit Board

*Once you have decided upon the circuit you intend to use you will need to decide how to solder it together permanently. There are several ways of building circuit boards.*

*You do not need to know all of the methods in detail but you should be able to explain one making process with which you are familiar.*

## From Circuit Diagram to Working Circuit

Before making a permanent version of a circuit, especially one with which you or your teacher are not familiar, it is worth testing whether it works by building it on prototype board (see page 44). Once you are sure that the circuit is suitable for its intended purpose you then need to design the circuit board.

Whichever method you use you will need to think carefully how you will make the connections between the circuit components. Try not to make your boards too big but make sure that you leave enough room for the components. You might find it helps to collect the components together first to help you decide how much space you need.

The two methods shown here are suitable for quick prototypes of your circuit, but you should use a PCB to produce a more durable version (page 132).

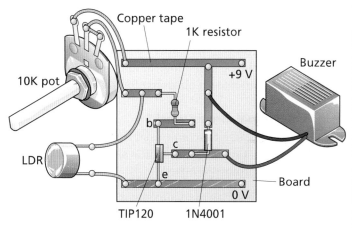

## Using Copper Tape

4 mm wide self-adhesive copper tape can be used to make simple circuit boards. The tape is stuck onto a backing board, card, styrene, etc. and the components are soldered onto the tape. This is a simple form of surface mounting. It is quick and easy, and does not require the use of special equipment. However, it is only suitable for simple circuits and for developing prototypes.

You will need to solder across tape junctions to make sure the circuit is complete.

## Stripboard

Stripboard is plastic sheet with a grid of holes linked by copper strips. It can be used to build prototype circuits without needing to use chemicals to process the board. The spacing of the holes is commonly 0.1 inch which makes it easy to locate the component legs.

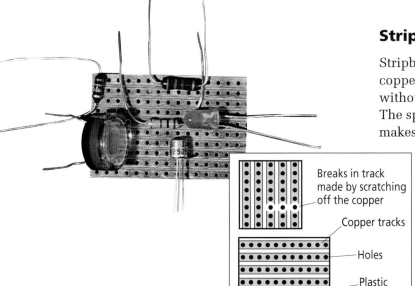

Breaks in track made by scratching off the copper

Copper tracks

Holes

Plastic board

Circuits built on prototype board can be transferred easily to stripboard. If you hold the stripboard with the copper strips as the 'Y axis' then the circuit layout should be similar.

Remember that the copper acts as the connecting tracks. You will need to break the tracks at certain points to make sure that the components are not 'shorted out' by the track.

# Fault Finding

*If your circuit doesn't work properly after you have assembled and soldered it, you will need to carry out a series of fault-finding checks to isolate the problem(s).*

Most problems are caused by poor circuit design or construction. You will probably be more successful if you approach the task in a logical manner. Use the following questions as a checklist for your circuit.

### Did the original circuit work?

If you or your teacher haven't used the circuit before you should test whether it works as it is supposed to by first building it on prototype board.

First carry out a series of visual checks.

### Is my soldering good?

Look for dry joints, solder bridging across tracks, etc. What do you think is meant by a 'dry joint'?

### Do the circuit board connections match the schematic circuit?

Check through logically – perhaps left to right.

### Are there any obvious breaks in the circuit board tracks where there shouldn't be?

On PCB boards, narrow tracks in particular tend to get broken due to scratching and over-etching when making the board.

Use a multi-meter or logic probe to check.

### Is the battery/power supply giving the correct voltage to the circuit?

With a multimeter set on d.c. volts, check that the lines from the power supply give the expected voltage and polarity when connected to the circuit.

### Have you used the correct components?

Are they in the correct places and the right way round? A common error is to use the wrong value resistors – you should check the values using the colour code (see page 65). Putting diodes, transistors, ICs and capacitors in the wrong way round is another source of error.

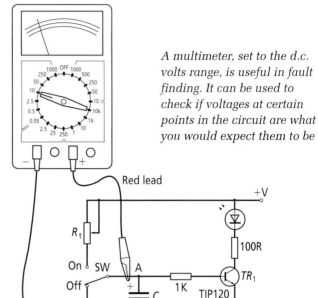

*A multimeter, set to the d.c. volts range, is useful in fault finding. It can be used to check if voltages at certain points in the circuit are what you would expect them to be*

### ■ ACTIVITY

▶ Build up the circuit as shown on prototype board.

▶ If you connect a multimeter to the capacitor contacts (use d.c. volt setting with probe leads as shown), the meter reading should increase gradually once the switch is in the 'on' position.

▶ Try to measure the voltage at which the transistor switches on. What should it be?

▶ Make a note of the voltage value. Do you think it would be the same for all transistors? Try to find out.

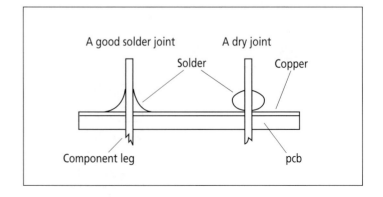

# Making It and Final Evaluation

*As you develop the electronics you will also have to design a container for the circuit you have made, and to evaluate your work.*

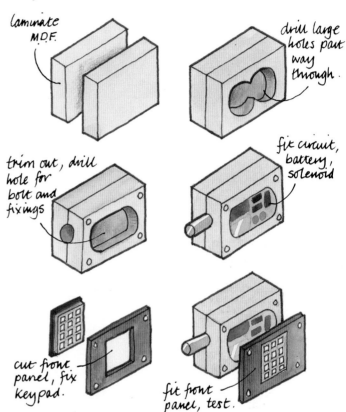

laminate M.D.F.

drill large holes part way through.

trim out, drill hole for bolt and fixings

fit circuit, battery, solenoid

cut front panel, fix keypad.

fit front panel, test.

## Containers

If you choose to take the lock through to production you will find valuable information in the section beginning on page 97.

## Evaluating Your Solution

▷ How easy will it be to fit the lock to conventional equipment?

▷ How could it be modified to make it useful in a variety of applications?

▷ How simple is it for the operator to use the lock?

▷ What happens if the operator forgets the code?

▷ How easy is it to reprogramme the code?

▷ Could the alarm 'lockout' be more effective?

To find the answers to these questions you will need to get a number of people to try out your design. Make a careful note of what they do and what they say.

## Improving Your Design

How could your basic electronic solution be developed further to produce an even better design?

▷ Circuits could be used to connect up the remaining keys of a pad to make it more difficult to find the right combination.

▷ A timing circuit could relock the door after a set time. Timing circuits are discussed on pages 62–64. A relay used as a latch (see page 47) would hold the bolt back until the device is reset.

▷ Would a sound as each button is pressed help the user?

▷ A more sophisticated system could sense when each switch is pressed in sequence. This will require logic gates to be connected to components called bistables. See pages 86–87 for more information on bistables.

▷ Are the materials used to construct the lock casing strong enough?

▷ How could the lock container be made more appealing? What finish would last the longest?

# Examination Questions

*You should spend about one and a half hours answering the following questions. To complete the paper you will need some A4 paper, basic drawing equipment, and colouring materials. You are reminded of the need for good English and clear presentation in your answers.*

**1.** This question is about the design of electronic products.
*(Total 12 marks)* See pages 6-31.

a) Give two examples of modern electronic products and explain how they have changed our lives.
*(4 marks)*

b) Why would the manufacturer carry out a product analysis of products from other companies?
*(1 mark)*

c) When starting to design a new product the manufacturer will carry out market research. How can ICT be used in market research and what benefits does it bring?
*(4 marks)*

d) Computer Aided Design (CAD) is now widely used in the design and manufacturing industry. Explain a specific example where CAD is used in the electronics industry and the benefits it will bring. *(3 marks)*

**2.** This question is about systems.
*(Total 12 marks)* See pages 14-15.

a) What are the three sub-systems found in all control systems?
*(3 marks)*

b) Domestic burglar alarms are widely used today. What function does each of the following sub-systems perform in such an alarm?
*(3 marks)*

    i) Arming Switch
    ii) Delay
    iii) Transducer driver

c) Use these sub-systems to help you draw the complete system diagram for a burglar alarm.
*(6 marks)*

**3.** This question is about Logic.
*(Total 7 marks)* See pages 40-43.

To disarm the alarm when using a keypad requires the use of an AND logic gate.

a) What function does an AND gate perform? *(1 mark)*

b) Draw the truth table for an AND gate. *(2 marks)*

c) The keypad will also use a NOT gate. Explain the function of a NOT gate. *(1 mark)*

d) Draw the truth table for an Exclusive OR gate. *(3 marks)*

**4.** This question is about relays and output devices. *(Total 8 marks)* See pages 46-49.

a) The 24-volt siren will be switched on by using a relay. Why is the siren not connected directly to an IC? *(1 mark)*

b) Draw the circuit diagram for the sub-system that contains the relay and show how it is connected to the IC. *(3 marks)*

c) The manufacturer considered using a 9-volt siren and FET. Draw the circuit diagram for this sub-system and explain what are the advantages this solution gives. *(4 marks)*

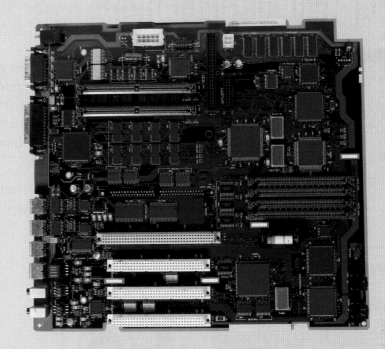

**5.** This question is about circuit construction. *(Total 8 marks)* See pages 50-53.

a) Before you assemble your circuit by soldering the components how could you ensure that it will operate as you want? *(2 marks)*

b) There are three different ways you could make your circuit board. What are these different methods of construction and what are the advantages of each method? *(6 marks)*

**6.** This question is about fault finding. *(Total 3 marks)* See pages 50-53.

a) While the manufacturer's first prototype worked, some of the circuits would not work when mass-produced. One of the problems was broken tracks on the PCB. How could this be checked for before any components were soldered in place? *(1 mark)*

b) Some circuits suffered from dry joints. What do you understand by the term dry joint and what may have caused this? *(2 marks)*

Total marks = 50

# Project Two: Introduction

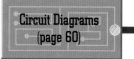

Circuit Diagrams
(page 60)

*A toothbrush manufacturer plans to produce a promotional gift to launch its new product range. It has developed the idea of a timer enclosed in a casing which will count three minutes – the minimum length of time children should spend cleaning their teeth.*

*Design and make a suitable electronic timer. Cost out the design and explain the electronics involved.*

Joining Circuits
(page 72)

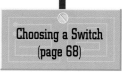

Choosing a Switch
(page 68)

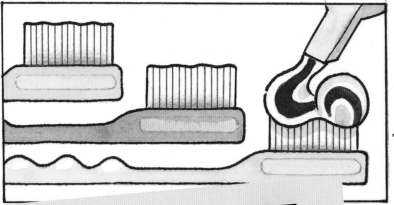

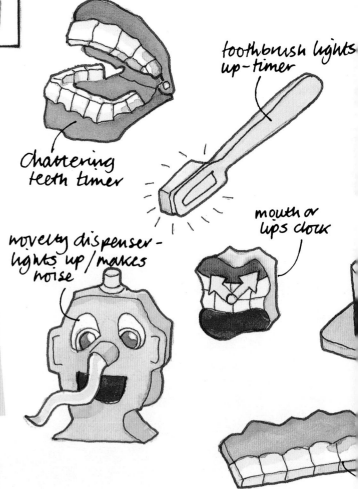

toothbrush lights up - timer

chattering teeth timer

mouth or lips clock

novelty dispenser - lights up / makes noise

```
Memo

From: The Marketing Director

To: The Design Team


Please make an immediate start on the
development of the promotional timer and
casing.

The product should show the company logo
clearly. A high quality of appearance and
finish is needed so that children will want to
use it. It should last in daily use for a year
without the need for maintainance. The design
will need to be costed out, and we will need a
full explanation of the the electronics
involved.

The order will be for 5000 units which will
need to be manufactured at a very competitive
price. The target figure for the cost of
components for manufacture is under £2.
```

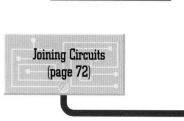

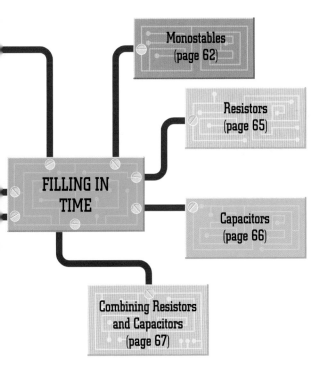

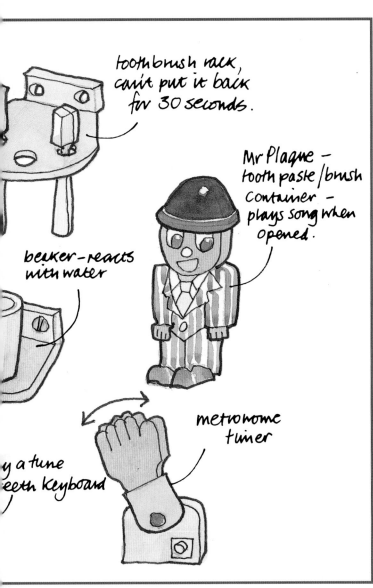

toothbrush rack, can't put it back for 30 seconds.

Mr Plaque - tooth paste/brush container - plays song when opened.

beaker - reacts with water

metronome timer

...y a tune ...eeth Keyboard

## Starting Questions

Before you start designing you will need to have a good understanding of the sorts of timing devices which could be used. What must you find out more about before you can write a successful design specification?

### The timer
▷ How accurate will the timer need to be?
▷ How large are other timers available on the market?
▷ Are there any novel ideas for timers on the market?

### The 'time-up' warning
▷ What type of warning would be suitable? Should it be a visual or an audible warning?
▷ Would it be useful to show intervals of time passing, or simply to indicate the end of the period?

### The electronics
▷ What will the electronics need to do?
▷ What will trigger the timer to start?
▷ Will the electronic control circuit provide enough current to drive the output device?
▷ What voltage will the output need to make it operate?
▷ How long will the warning need to be on for?

Page 14 shows how a systems approach to electronic design is useful.

▷ What will the power source be?
▷ How big will the power source be?
▷ How long will the power source need to last?

### The stand and logo
▷ What type of shape will the clients prefer?
▷ What materials will form the shapes required?
▷ What forming processes will be required?
▷ What are the costs for different types of sheet materials?
▷ What shape, size and colour is the company logo?

## First Thoughts/Further Investigation

Sketch your first ideas in response to the task. Show friends and members of your family your ideas.

What further information do you still need? Plan a programme of investigation to discover this information.

# Design Briefs and Specifications

*Designers start from a brief. When they have found out more about the needs of the user they prepare a specification – a very important list of the possibilities and restrictions of the final design.*

*A poorly written brief is likely to result in an inadequate specification. This in turn will lead to an unsuccessful design.*

A **design brief** is a general statement of what the company or a client requires, e.g. 'design an electronic timer which will appeal to children. It must be inexpensive enough to be given away as part of a product promotion'.

Before design development work can begin, the designer needs to undertake research to clarify and add detail to the brief.

Eventually the designer will be able to produce a **design specification** – a list of the possibilities and restrictions of the final design. It is important that the specification is as precise as possible to avoid costly mistakes, and it will usually be checked and approved by the client before development work proceeds. See page 20 of the Project Guide for more on writing a design specification.

## Writing Your Specification

It is essential that you consider the following aspects in your specification for the timer:

▷ what size it needs to be;
▷ what shape, colour, finish would appeal most to children;
▷ the most appropriate materials and production processes;
▷ any safety issues.

### Specification

✔ The timer will need to be accurate to within....
✔ The 'time-up' warning will need to be....
✔ The time period will be shown by....
✔ The electronics will need to....
✔ The power source must....
✔ The casing and the logo should....

### Research conclusions

The mother I spoke to showed me the bathroom cupboard she would probably keep the timer in. It had a narrow shelf which was only 100 mm deep. The shelf above was 150 mm away.

I showed my initial ideas to some young children. They liked the designs which had bright colours, and things that moved or made unexpected sounds.

## Designing by Numbers

Make sure you include numerical data in your specification. For example, 'the stand must be at least 60 mm wide and no more than 80 mm high to ensure stability'. Try to provide data for anything which can be measured, such as size, weight, quantity and life-time of the battery.

Also, when you are preparing a specification, don't forget that your designs will need to be suitable for a range of users who will have a variety of needs and preferences. For example, some children have larger hands than others. Some might prefer pastel colours while others go for bright primaries.

*To make the Psion personal organiser pocket-sized, the electronics had to be designed with the size and shape of the final casing firmly in mind*

## Design for life expectancy

Customers expect a product to work for a certain minimum time beyond the period of the guarantee. This time will vary according to the product.

A product which fails before the end of the guarantee period is going to be very costly to the manufacturer to repair. If a product needs expensive repair soon after the guarantee expires, a customer is unlikely to buy the same brand again, and it might develop a reputation for being unreliable.

However, if a product works successfully for many years consumers will not need to buy replacements so often, and demand will fall. The number of products made will drop, and as a result the price will rise. Many products therefore contain components which are likely to fail after a number of years, and which would be very expensive to repair or replace. This is known as 'planned obsolescence'.

A design specification needs to include information about how long the product should remain in working order, provided it is used and maintained by the consumer as instructed.

## Design for production

Products need to be designed to be easy to make. Some items may prove to be very difficult to make in quantity, however, perhaps because of their shape, the arrangement of their components or the materials required. Different manufacturing processes and materials can be used according to the numbers to be produced.

The rate of production is an important factor too. Producing 10 000 units by the end of the week in order to satisfy demand requires a very different approach to making the same number over a twelve-month period. There are also important implications if production needs to be organised in batches, for example 5000 this month and another 5000 in a year's time.

A design specification therefore needs to include details of the total number of units likely to be made, the production rates and, if appropriate, the sizes of batches.

Pages 126-143 explore planning for production in more detail.

## Design for maintenance

Designers need to consider how often a new product will need to be maintained during its usage.

They will also have to think about how easy it is to maintain. If a component needs cleaning, adjusting or replacing often by the user (e.g. replacing a battery) it must be quick and easy to do. Other work might need to be done by trained specialists, however, and providing easy access might result in damage if the user tries to do it themselves.

Ideally a product should be maintenance free, but this is likely to mean using more high quality components with narrower tolerances, which will inevitably increase the cost. When preparing a design specification, a statement needs to be made about how frequently and easily different parts of a product are likely to need maintenance.

# Circuit Diagrams

*Electronic circuits are usually drawn using symbols to represent the components. You may be familiar with some of them already. You need to be able to recognise all of the symbols shown on the right-hand page.*

It's a good idea to build up a library of component symbols in your word processor.

## Why Use Symbols?

Symbols are used because they simplify circuit drawing.

For example, an integrated circuit (IC) is drawn as a simple block:

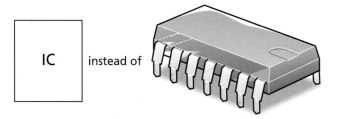

instead of

A double pole double throw slide switch is drawn:

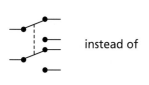

instead of

### KEY POINTS

- Symbols are used to represent electronic components.
- Connecting wires are usually drawn as straight lines.
- Connections are shown as a dot unless components are in line.

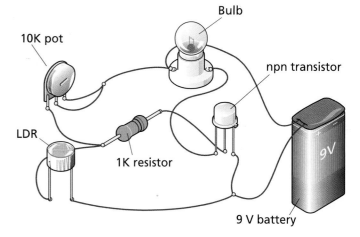

Components: 10K pot, Bulb, npn transistor, LDR, 1K resistor, 9 V battery

## Drawing Circuit Diagrams

When you draw a circuit, or schematic, diagram you should join the component symbols with straight lines. These represent the wires which link them to make up the circuit. You should draw a dot where components and/or conductors join. Note – if there is no dot it means that there is no connection, unless the components are in line.

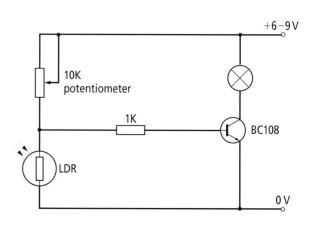

Circuit labels: +6–9 V, 10K potentiometer, 1K, BC108, LDR, 0 V

# Circuit Symbols

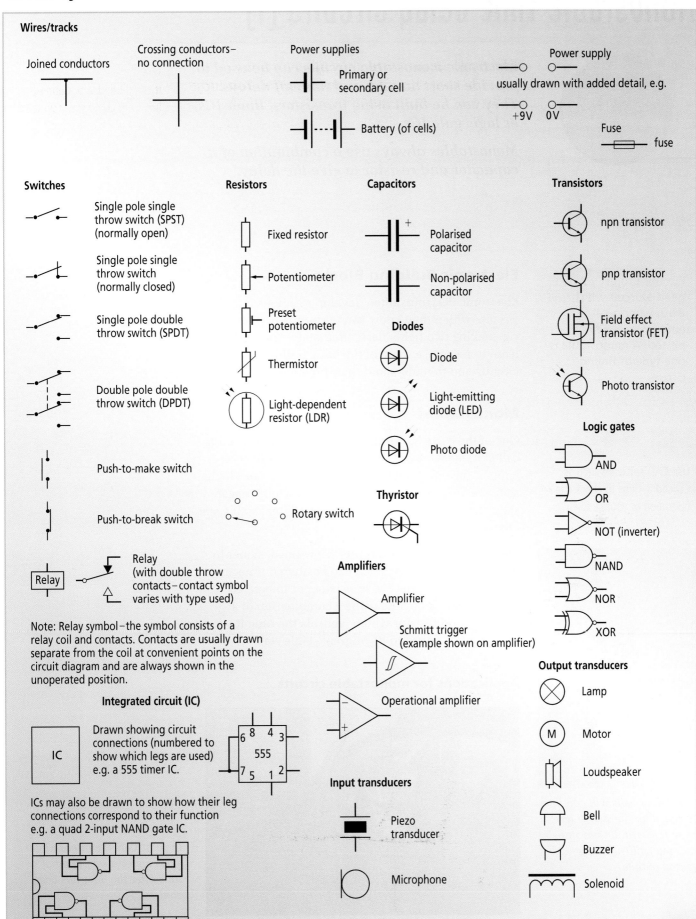

### Wires/tracks

Joined conductors

Crossing conductors– no connection

**Power supplies**

Primary or secondary cell

Battery (of cells)

**Power supply**

usually drawn with added detail, e.g.

+9V   0V

Fuse

fuse

### Switches

Single pole single throw switch (SPST) (normally open)

Single pole single throw switch (normally closed)

Single pole double throw switch (SPDT)

Double pole double throw switch (DPDT)

Push-to-make switch

Push-to-break switch

Rotary switch

Relay

Relay (with double throw contacts – contact symbol varies with type used)

Note: Relay symbol – the symbol consists of a relay coil and contacts. Contacts are usually drawn separate from the coil at convenient points on the circuit diagram and are always shown in the unoperated position.

### Integrated circuit (IC)

IC

Drawn showing circuit connections (numbered to show which legs are used) e.g. a 555 timer IC.

8  4
6       3
555
7  5  1  2

ICs may also be drawn to show how their leg connections correspond to their function e.g. a quad 2-input NAND gate IC.

### Resistors

Fixed resistor

Potentiometer

Preset potentiometer

Thermistor

Light-dependent resistor (LDR)

### Capacitors

+ Polarised capacitor

Non-polarised capacitor

### Diodes

Diode

Light-emitting diode (LED)

Photo diode

### Thyristor

### Amplifiers

Amplifier

Schmitt trigger (example shown on amplifier)

Operational amplifier

### Input transducers

Piezo transducer

Microphone

### Transistors

npn transistor

pnp transistor

Field effect transistor (FET)

Photo transistor

### Logic gates

AND

OR

NOT (inverter)

NAND

NOR

XOR

### Output transducers

Lamp

Motor

Loudspeaker

Bell

Buzzer

Solenoid

# Monostable Time Delay Circuits (1)

*Filling In Time*

*Electronic monostable circuits can be used to provide short time-on and time-off delays. They can be built using transistors, timer ICs or logic gate ICs.*

*Monostables always use a combination of a capacitor and resistor to give the delay.*

For this project you will need a circuit which will warn when a set amount of time has passed. A monostable is one type of timing circuit.

**ICT** ➡

Use CAD software such as Crocodile Clips to check the operation of your circuit.

## Electronic Building Blocks

Electronic designers often develop solutions out of circuits which they know can perform a particular task, e.g. making two lights flash alternately. You will need to learn to recognise some of the basic building block circuits and to understand their function.

## Monostables

One of the basic building blocks is a group of circuits called monostables. The name comes from the Greek 'monos' meaning single. A monostable has one stable state, i.e. off or on, until it is triggered. Once triggered its state changes but then returns to its original stable state after a certain time.

Electronic monostable circuits allow the designer to produce a time delay which can be altered if necessary. They can use a variety of transistors or integrated circuits, and all operate using a combination of a capacitor and resistor which controls the time it takes for the device to return to its original stable state.

## Applications for monostable circuits

*Some door bells will continue to ring after the switch has been released. It then stops automatically after a set period of time.*

*In some cars the interior light stays on for a set period of time after the door has been shut.*

## Solution One: A Simple Transistor-based Timer Circuit

Spring loaded push-to-make or push-to-break switches are examples of monostable devices. More sophisticated electronic monostables are often triggered by these types of switches

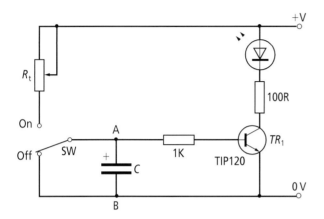

Do you understand all the symbols in the diagram below? Page 61 has a list of symbols to help you identify the components.

### How it works

The transistor switches on after a time delay once the switch is operated to the 'on' position. The time delay is controlled by the values of the resistor $R_t$ and the capacitor $C$. The capacitor charges via the variable resistor until the voltage at A is big enough to switch on the transistor $TR_1$. Pages 66-67 give more detail about resistors and capacitors.

## Solution Two: A Logic Gate Monostable

This monostable works by using logic gates beyond the resistor and capacitor network. The output goes 'high' after a delay controlled by $R_t$ and $C$ once the input is taken 'high'. (Note – the input has to be kept 'high' so a switch must latch 'on'.)

This circuit uses either NOR (4001) or NAND (4011) gates connected as NOT gates. Try to explain how it works. (See pages 42-43 for more information.)

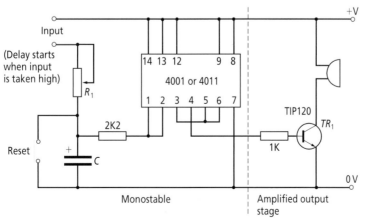

*Testing*

*If you connect a multimeter to the capacitor contacts (use d.c. volts setting with probe leads as shown), the meter reading should increase gradually once the switch is in the 'on' position*

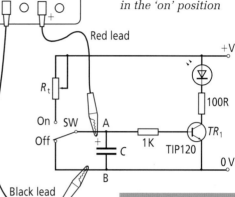

Red lead

Black lead

### ▥ ACTIVITY

Using $C$=1000 μF and $R_t$= 100K, try to measure the voltage at which the transistor switches on. What should it be? Make a note of the voltage value. Do you think it would be the same for all transistors? Try to find out.

### IN YOUR PROJECT

▶ If your design needs a set period of time to elapse after a switch is pushed, then you will need an electronic monostable rather than a simple switch.

▶ A transistor-based timer is a cheap, simple and reliable circuit. Its main disadvantage is that the transistor tends to switch on gradually rather than having a definite on/off action.

▶ A better switching action can be achieved using logic gates which also have the advantage of extending battery life.

▶ Most IC circuits need an additional amplifier or transducer-driver stage to power buzzers or other output devices.

▶ Pages 46-48 have details of transducer-driver building block circuits.

# Monostable Time Delay Circuits (2)

## Solution Three: Using a 555 Timer IC Monostable

An alternative to using a transistor or logic gates to make monostables is to use a 555 timer IC. The chip contains quite a complex circuit. As a designer you only need to know how to control the output with a variety of inputs.

When the circuit is connected as shown below the LED will light and the buzzer sound once the input switch is pressed. They will stay on for a set time and then switch off. The buzzer is switched on and off through a transistor amplifier stage.

The output from pin 3 stays 'high' for a time controlled by the values of the resistor $R_t$ and the capacitor $C$.

**IN YOUR PROJECT**

A 555 is a well-known and reliable timer circuit. However, it has the disadvantage of needing an amplifier to drive some output devices.

The length of the delay can be calculated using the formula $T = 1.1 R_t \times C$. This is the time required for the capacitor to charge to 2/3 of $V_{CC}$. For a circuit using a 9 V supply it would be the time to charge to 6V.

Page 67 will help with calculating delay times.

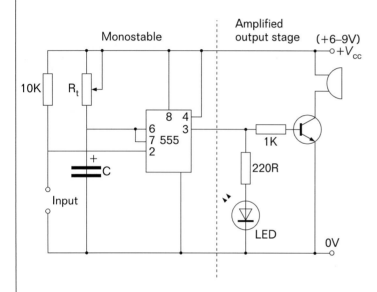

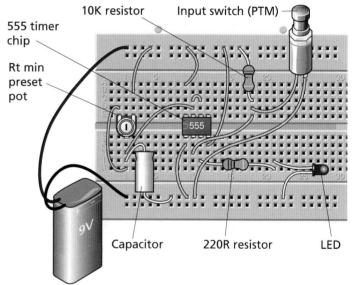

*Prototype board layout for 555 timer IC monostable*

■ **ACTIVITY**

Build some of the monostable circuits. Write a short report on each one which covers the following points:

▶ How easy was it to adjust the time delay?
▶ How accurately could you time a minute?
▶ Try to explain how it works and how effective you felt it was in use.
▶ How efficient is it at conserving the battery?
▶ Did they take different times to construct?
▶ Which do you think will be the easiest to manufacture?
▶ Make up a table to show the advantages and disadvantages of each circuit.

Use an electronics catalogue to help you calculate the component cost for a production run of 5000 units.

**KEY POINTS**

● Building block circuits can be combined to make other circuits.
● Monostable building blocks are used to switch an output for a set length of time.
● Monostables can be made from transistors, timer ICs such as the 555 and logic gates such as NAND and NOR gates.

# Resistors

*Resistance is a property of materials which determines how easily charge can flow through them at a particular voltage. Resistance is measured in units called* ohms.

*This is the symbol for ohms*

## Fixed Resistors

Resistors are made in a range of values known as the preferred values series (see page 127).

Most of the fixed resistors you are likely to use will only be suitable for use with small currents. They are likely to be 0.25 W, 0.33 W or 0.5 W resistors. This is a measure of the maximum power-handling capacity.

## Resistor Colour Code

Most resistors are labelled with four coloured bands to show the resistance value and tolerance. This is known as the resistor colour code. You should know how to use it to check resistor values.

## Tolerance

Tolerance is a measure of the accuracy of the colour coding in indicating the actual resistance of the resistor. For example, a 1K gold band resistor – 5% tolerance could have a resistance of 1000 ohms ± 50 ohms (that is from 950 to 1050 ohms).

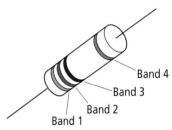

Band 4
Band 3
Band 2
Band 1

| Colour | Band 1 | Band 2 | Band 3 (multiplier) | Band 4 (tolerance) |
|--------|--------|--------|---------------------|--------------------|
| Black  | -      | 0      | None                |                    |
| Brown  | 1      | 1      | 0                   |                    |
| Red    | 2      | 2      | 00                  |                    |
| Orange | 3      | 3      | 000                 |                    |
| Yellow | 4      | 4      | 0000                |                    |
| Green  | 5      | 5      | 00000               |                    |
| Blue   | 6      | 6      | 000000              |                    |
| Violet | 7      | 7      | -                   |                    |
| Grey   | 8      | 8      | -                   |                    |
| White  | 9      | 9      | -                   |                    |
| Gold   | -      | -      | 0.1                 | 5%                 |
| Silver | -      | -      | 0.01                | 10%                |

## Variable Resistors (Potentiometer)

The resistance value is changed by moving the wiper along the resistance track. The maximum value is usually printed on the body.

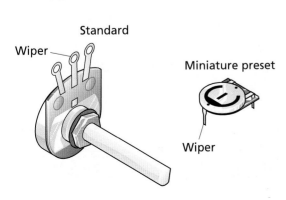

Standard

Wiper

Miniature preset

Wiper

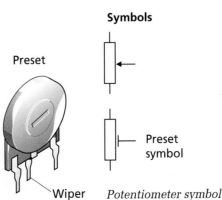

Preset

Wiper

**Symbols**

Preset symbol

*Potentiometer symbol*

■ **ACTIVITY**

Use the colour code to work out the resistance of five different fixed resistors. Check their actual resistances using a multimeter set on ohms (see page 134). Are the readings within the tolerance?

# Capacitors

*Capacitors store electrical energy by separating positive and negative electrical charges. When the capacitor is charged up there is a voltage between the two leads, in the same way as a battery has a voltage across its terminals.*

## Polarised capacitors

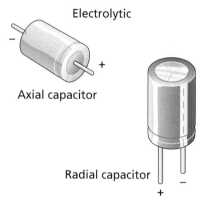

Electrolytic

Axial capacitor

Radial capacitor

## Non-polarised capacitors
### Common types

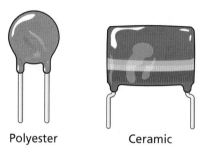

Polyester      Ceramic

■ **ACTIVITY**

Learn to identify different types of capacitors.

It is important to be able to recognise polarised capacitors because they must be connected the correct way round in a circuit to work effectively.

You will usually use polarised capacitors in timer circuits.

Find out what these terms mean:

► microfarad (μF)
► nanofarad (nF)
► picofarad (pF)
► polarised.

Circuit symbols

Non-polarised capacitor

Polarised capacitor

If the leads are connected together in a circuit, the capacitor discharges its stored electrical energy and, like a battery, produces an electric current.

Capacitors come in many shapes and sizes. Their ability to store quantities of charge at a particular voltage is called the **capacitance**. The capacitance is measured in units called farads (the symbol is F). The farad is a very large unit so capacitors used in electronic circuits are often rated in micro-, nano- or picofarads.

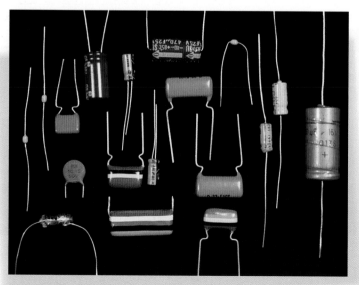

# Combining Resistors and Capacitors

*Resistors and capacitors are normally available only in 'preferred values' (a limited range of values). To create different values, resistors and capacitors can be linked together. You can use the formulae below to calculate the total value of two or more resistors or capacitors connected together in series or parallel.*

ICT

You could use a spreadsheet to design a simple time constant calculator.

## ■ ACTIVITY

▶ What do you think is meant by 'leakage'? Try to find out.

▶ Tantalum capacitors leak less than electrolytic capacitors but are only available in values up to around 100 μF. Try to find out how longer delays are achieved.

▶ What value resistor would give a delay of 5 seconds when used with a 100 μF capacitor?

▶ Find out how to use a spreadsheet to calculate time constants. This can make it easier and quicker to find the right combination of resistors and capacitors.

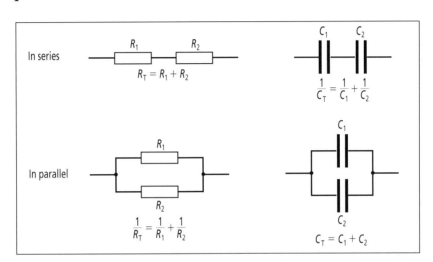

In series
$$R_T = R_1 + R_2$$

$$\frac{1}{C_T} = \frac{1}{C_1} + \frac{1}{C_2}$$

In parallel
$$\frac{1}{R_T} = \frac{1}{R_1} + \frac{1}{R_2}$$

$$C_T = C_1 + C_2$$

## Resistor/Capacitor Circuits

A resistor and a capacitor connected together are often referred to as an RC circuit. R stands for the resistance of the resistor and C for the capacitance of the capacitor.

A resistor, used in combination with a capacitor, can control the length of time it takes for the capacitor to charge or discharge.

The time delay (on or off) of a monostable circuit, such as those on pages 62-64, is known as the time constant. The size of the delay depends upon the values of the timer capacitor and resistor.

### IN YOUR PROJECT

Monostables are only suitable for delays of up to a few minutes. If high-value resistor/capacitor combinations are used the capacitor tends to lose charge by leakage and the time delay becomes inaccurate.

The time constant ($T$ in seconds) can be made equal to the resistor value ($R$ in ohms) × the capacitor value ($C$ in farads), e.g. for a 1000 μF capacitor used with a 100K resistor:

$$T = 100\,000 \times \frac{1000}{1\,000\,000} \text{ seconds}$$

$$= 100 \text{ seconds}$$

Or

$$T \text{ (seconds)} = R \text{ (M ohms)} \times C \text{ (micro farads)}$$
$$T = 0.1 \times 1000$$
$$T = 100 \text{ seconds}$$

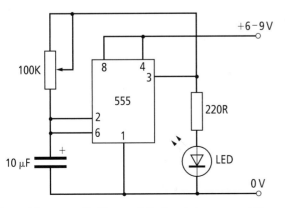

*A 555 IC astable controlled by an RC circuit (see page 90)*

# Choosing a Suitable Switch

*Finding the right switch for your design is important. It is usually the first thing the user tries. If a switch is difficult or annoying to operate it is unlikely that the person will want to go on using the product.*

## Mechanical Switches

The mechanical switches shown below are commonly used in electronic products to switch the device on or off by 'making' or 'breaking' the power supply circuit.

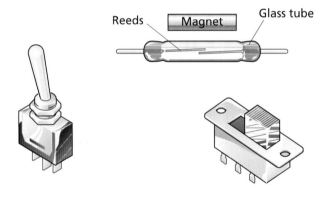

Switches are described by their method of operation, the number of poles and the number of throws. Common types are:

▷ single pole single throw (SPST);
▷ single pole double throw (SPDT); and
▷ double pole double throw (DPDT).

They are operated in a variety of ways such as slide, toggle, rocker, push, key, micro, rotary, membrane and tilt.

Some switches can also be used to divert the current path into one or more directions (ways or throws), and are able to control more than one circuit at once.

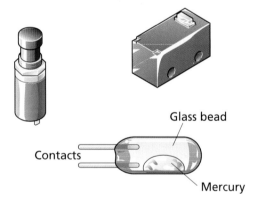

## Touch Switches

Touch switches are triggered by a small electric current which flows when the skin acts as a conductor. They work best with ICs which trigger with little current, as the skin has a high resistance.

## A Logic Gate Touch Switch

A simple, but sensitive, touch switch can be made using a 2-input NAND gate as shown in the diagram.

### How it works

A NAND gate provides a 'high' output if one or both of its inputs is 'low'. In the circuit shown, both inputs are connected to +V and are therefore 'high', making output 'low'. If the touch plates are bridged the input connected to them is connected to 0 V, via the skin, which takes it 'low'. The output therefore switches to 'high' or 'on'.

Logic gates are digital devices which require very little current to operate them, making them ideal for this type of sensing. The output is low powered and needs to be connected into one of the monostable circuits in your design.

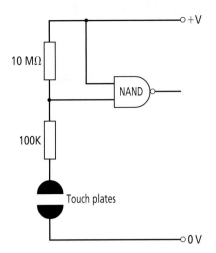

*NAND gate touch switch*

## FET Touch Switch

A sensitive touch switch can be built using an FET (field effect transistor) as shown in the diagrams.

An FET makes a better touch switch than a bipolar transistor because it has a **digital** switching action – once an FET is triggered by an input it turns on fully. Bipolar transistors turn on gradually – the collector/emitter current increases as the base current increases. This is known as an **analogue** switching action. See page 48 for more information on FETs.

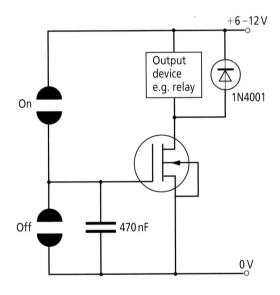

*FET touch switch – latching version*

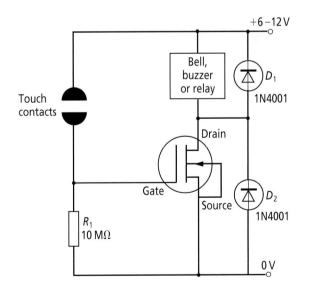

*FET touch switch – non-latching version*

**IN YOUR PROJECT**

You may need a very sensitive switch which will not require any pressure to operate it.

These 'touch switches' are very popular with electronic designers since they feel better in use than the normal 'pressure switches'.

## Other Sensors

Switches which sense changes, such as in light or temperature, are used with a resistor in an arrangement called a **potential divider**. There is more information on potential dividers on page 84.

# Taking Things Further

*If you want to gain a high grade for your project it is important that it is complex enough and finished to a high standard. You will also need to design a container for you circuit. These are explored further on pages 70, 71 and 74.*

## Using Two Process Blocks

A simple circuit such as an egg timer uses just one process block. However if you combine two process blocks in your project you can create a more complex circuit that can potentially gain you a higher grade. An example would be an electronic dice that combines an astable circuit with a counter.

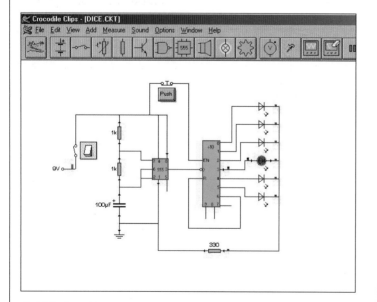

To find out more about circuits, go to:
www.circuitcit.com

## Circuit Development

It is important to show all stages of the design for your circuit. You should show how a variety of simple circuits could be combined to form a more complex circuit and how alternative circuits could be used to achieve the same outcome.

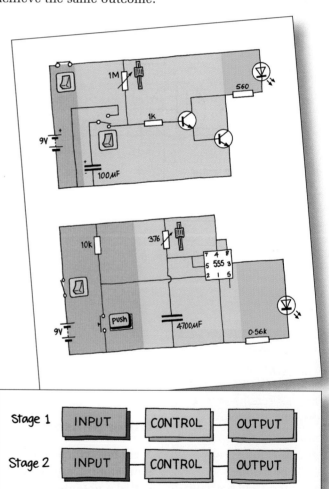

## Assembling your Circuit in the Case

The quality of construction will influence your final grade. Flying leads should be sleeved with heat shrink where they are soldered to LED's and other components. You should consider how your battery would be held in the case. It is possible to use a battery holder that solders directly to your PCB or make one from a piece of acrylic. Once your circuit is working it must be firmly held in the projects case. You can do this by using a short length of plastic tube, such as an old pen or by using commercially available fixings.

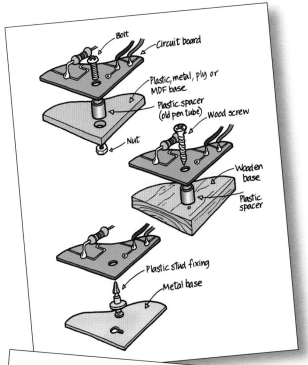

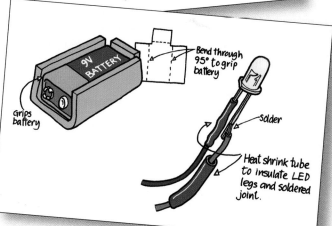

## Selecting Components

Careful selection of components will help improve the quality of your project. An example would be using a round switch rather than a square one, as it is easier to drill a round hole rather than cut a square one in the case.

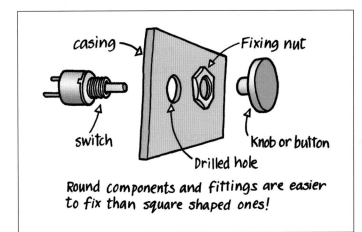

Round components and fittings are easier to fix than square shaped ones!

### ■ ACTIVITY

1 Design a timing circuit that will make an LED flash on and off every second, for a period of 30 seconds after it has been triggered.
2 Design a timing circuit that will make a 24-volt motor come on for 20 seconds.
3 Use a component catalogue to identify a range of different switches. Explain which ones would be useful in your project and which are unsuitable. Give reasons for your choice.

### IN YOUR PROJECT

Plan how you are going fit your circuit and battery in the project case. Draw out where each part will go to ensure there is enough space.

CAD can be used to move the parts around on screen to plan the initial layout of a product.

### KEY POINTS

- If you want to achieve a high grade ensure you use two process blocks in your circuit.
- Ensure the detail aspects of your project are well finished.
- Consider what components you will use and how these will help improve the quality of your project.

# Joining Circuits

*When producing electronic products it is often very difficult to just use a single building block circuit, such as a monostable. Many designs will involve combining two or more basic building blocks.*

*When circuits are combined it is often possible to redesign them to reduce the number of components.*

## Simplifying the Circuit

One solution to the timer circuit is to combine a touch switch with a monostable circuit.

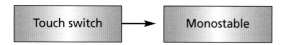

Combining these two building block circuits gives a practical example of some of the problems you might encounter when developing solutions to your design problems.

If you look at the information on pages 62-69 you will see that there are a number of possible touch switch circuits and monostable circuits.

One way to make a touch switch is to use a NAND gate (see page 69). NAND gates can also be used to make a monostable, and since NAND gate ICs often consist of four gates in one DIL package it would be possible to use one chip to make both circuits.

The 4011 quad 2-input NAND gate IC can be used to make practical versions of both a touch switch and a monostable, as shown in these circuit diagrams.

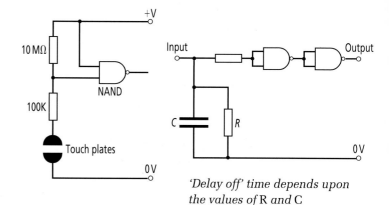

*'Delay off' time depends upon the values of R and C*

## Combining the Circuits

The circuits for the monostable and touch switch could be combined to make a touch switch with a 'delay off'. This means it holds the output 'high' for a set time.

Both circuits use the same IC, and since only three NAND gates are needed in total it is possible to make both from one IC. This saving of components is important in industry since it saves on material and labour costs.

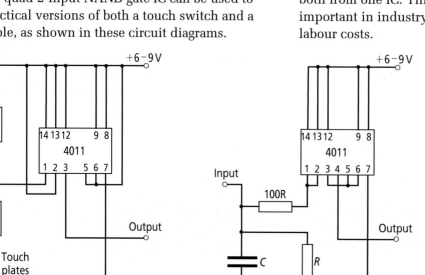

### ■ ACTIVITY

Build the two circuits shown on the left separately, and test them. Then build the combined circuit shown at the top of the next page. Compare the amount of time it takes to build the two separate circuits with the single IC solution.

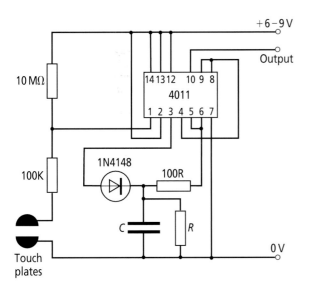

## Adding a Transducer-Driver

The use of the logic gate chip helps to produce a digital switching action. The output is low powered, however, and you may need to add a transducer-driver to allow the circuit to control a suitable output device. Pages 46-49 offer a number of transducer-driver circuits.

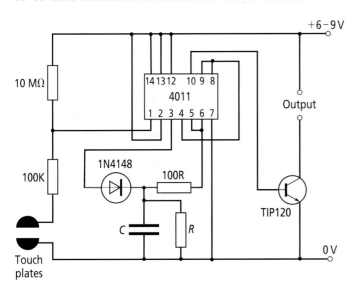

## KEY POINTS

- NAND gates can be used to make switches and monostables.
- Building blocks can be combined to make other circuits.
- A single logic gate IC can be used to make two circuits (component redundancy).
- The output of ICs often needs amplification by a transducer-driver.

## How It Works

The output from the touch switch is 'high' when the touch plates are bridged across the skin. This charges the capacitor and also produces a 'high' at the output of the monostable. When the input is removed the output stays 'on' for a short time as the capacitor discharges through the resistor $R$ and the two NAND gates.

### Why is there a diode in the circuit?

The 1N4148 diode has been added to the junction of the touch switch output and monostable input. This is necessary since the touch switch output goes 'low' when the input is removed. This would discharge the capacitor if not for the diode, which prevents the current flow back through the touch switch.

## ■ ACTIVITY

When developing your product, you will need to move from the prototype board towards a more permanent soldered circuit. This will be more typical of the size of the electronics in the finished product.

If you wish to make up this circuit using a permanent method, see page 47 for details of how to process the board.

The diagrams below show a possible PCB mask and component layout (scale x1) of the combined circuit and transducer-driver.

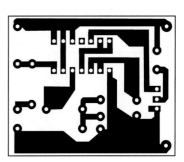

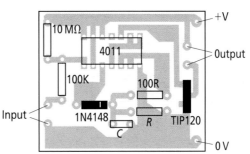

# Designing the Container

*When the electronics system has been finalised, you will need to start developing a suitable container. It will need to be visually attractive to appeal to children, but also protect the circuits from water and in everyday use.*

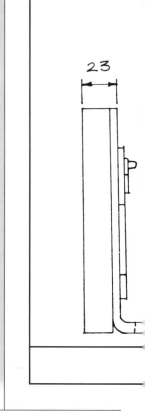

23

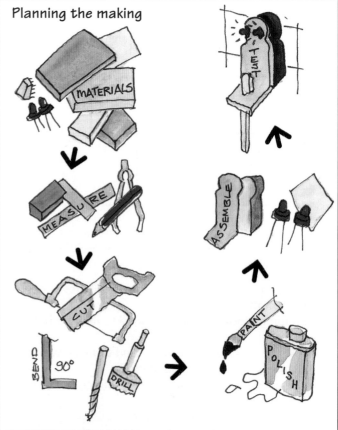

Planning the making

MATERIALS

MEASURE

CUT

BEND 90°

DRILL

TEST

ASSEMBLE

PAINT

POLISH

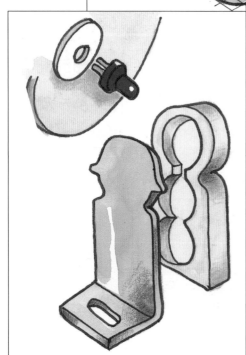

# Testing and Evaluation

You could use a spreadsheet to record your results and present them using the graph facility.

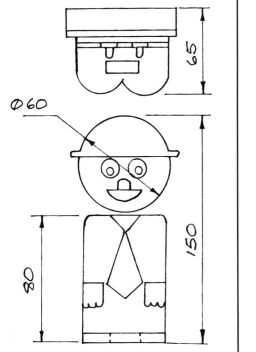

## Testing the Timer

Show the product to a number of different people. Record their comments.

Ask about its visual appeal. Do they find it eye-catching? What do they think about the colour? How easy is to turn on the timer? Is the company logo clearly visible?

Run a test of the timer. How accurate is it? Compare it with an accurate clock and record the exact time it took, say, for 20 timings. Show the results in a bar chart.

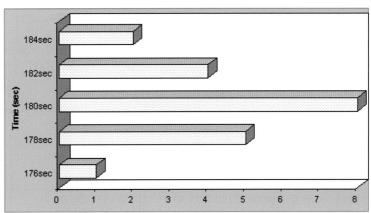

*Are you satisfied with this accuracy?*

## Final Evaluation

While evaluating your container design consider visual appeal, ease of use and accuracy of timing in particular. Refer directly to your final testing when discussing the successes and failures of your design.

Make sure you also comment on the process of development you went through.

▷ Did you do enough research into timing devices and the sorts of things which would appeal to children?
▷ Did you experiment widely enough with a range of circuit designs?
▷ Did you test a prototype? What did you learn from it?
▷ Did you finish the making on time? If not, how could your planning be improved?
▷ Is your final product made to a high standard of finish?

# Project Three: Introduction

*We all rely on a variety of alarms to warn of potential danger, protect our property, wake us up or tell us that our meal is ready. In this project you are asked to design and make an electronic alarm.*

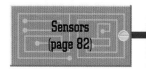

Sensors
(page 82)

Power Supplies
(page 94)

Operational Amplifiers
(page 92)

Alarm circuits are found in thousands of different products. It is now common for people to protect their property such as houses and cars with alarms. Alarms are also widely found as part of other electrical or electronic systems such as monitoring equipment in hospitals. Here, alarms are designed to warn of potential problems such as a low pulse rate, a change in temperature or a drop in blood pressure.

## The Task

Acme Alarms is a small production company which specialises in the manufacture of electronic products. It has asked you to design and produce a series of prototypes for a range of distinctive alarms to compete in small and specialised 'niche' markets.

## First Thoughts

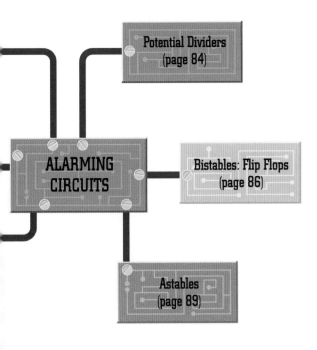

Potential Dividers
(page 84)

ALARMING
CIRCUITS

Bistables: Flip Flops
(page 86)

Astables
(page 89)

## Investigation

Make a list of alarms and electronic indicators that you have used or seen.

▷ What do they have in common?
▷ How do they communicate their message to you?

Visit local DIY stores to examine products that are currently available. Where possible, collect leaflets to find out more about popular alarms.

## Identifying a Need

Choose an area of interest such as fishing, personal safety, children or bicycles which appeals to you. Think through how an alarm could be of use.

▷ How much would people be willing to pay for an alarm?
▷ Are there alarms already on the market?
▷ How will yours be different?

Talk to someone who would use the alarm to discover what design features they would be looking for.

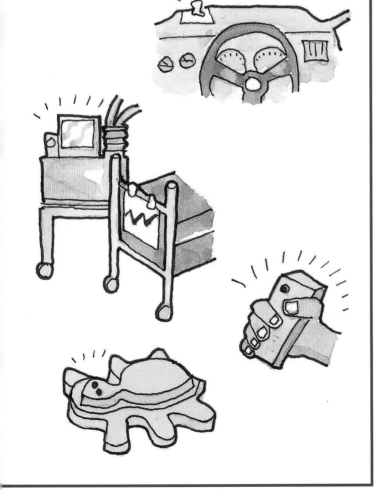

# Evaluating Existing Products

*You are about to design an alarm which is targeted on a particular market. To be successful you will need to look closely at what other designers and manufacturers are producing. Your research and evaluation of existing products will need to be comprehensive and systematic.*

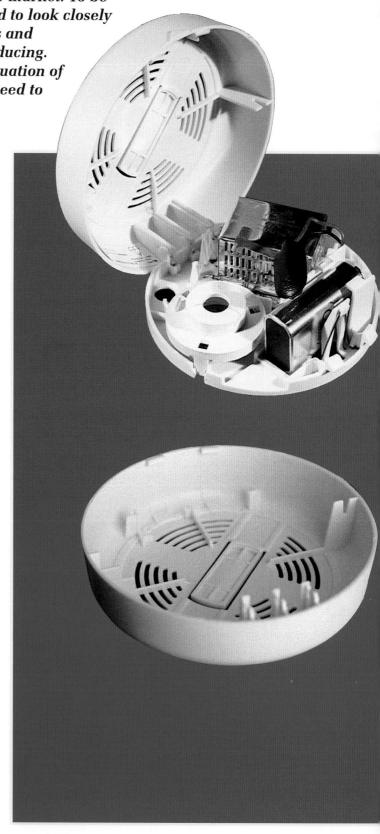

## Saving Lives

Smoke alarms are now part of our lives and yet only a few years ago very few people had installed them in their homes. The demand for a cheap and effective alarm was created when people became aware of the increasing numbers of fires where an early warning could have saved lives.

The technology involved in building smoke detectors has been available for many years. They work by 'sensing' the small particles which make up smoke in two ways. In the first method, the smoke particles interrupt a light beam which is shining on a detector.

The second method is more sensitive and uses ionising detectors. A weak radioactive source ionises the air in a chamber. The positive and negative ions produced are attracted to charged plates, resulting in a small current in the detector circuit. Minute charged smoke particles attract the ions and so lower the current. A comparator circuit checks the difference between two chambers and triggers the alarm if there is a difference. Find out more about comparators on page 92.

## ■ ACTIVITY

Prepare a case study for the alarm you would like to develop. Collect information under as many of the following headings as possible:

- size
- power supply
- price
- potential market (size, life style)

- how it works
- electronic components
- materials
- production methods
- packaging and promotion
- user comments
- social impact
- consumer demand.

## The Product Life Cycle

Products are not intended to last for ever, and have a life cycle which usually lasts over a period of years.

When a new product is first launched sales are likely to be slow. Profits from initial sales are unlikely to provide a return on the development, mass manufacture and initial promotion costs. Demand picks up as the product becomes known and accepted as worthwhile. Everyone starts to want one, and sales repay the initial investment and show a healthy profit.

In the third phase the product will be well established and selling well with minimum promotion, but also starting to compete with models being produced by other companies which may be cheaper or have a better performance specification.

In the final phase, sales will drop off, sometimes rapidly, as other products in their second and third phases begin to dominate the market. The cost of production may exceed the potential profit, so the model is withdrawn. Sometimes manufacturers relaunch products with minor modifications to help extend the sales period.

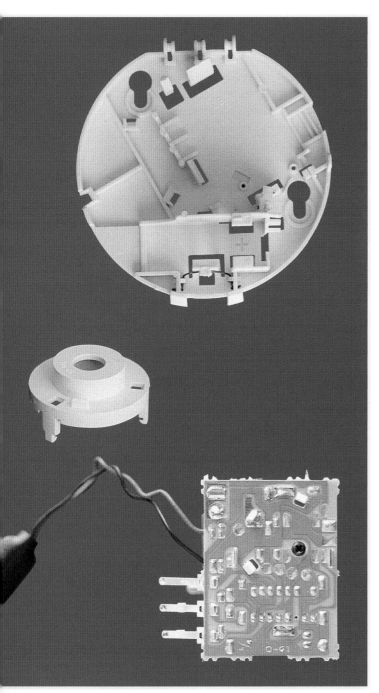

Most design is evolutionary. New products are rarely completely new, but an adaptation of an existing design, incorporating new features or using a number of different materials and components to produce a better-looking, better-working model which is cheaper to manufacture.

What stage do you think the alarm you are studying is at in terms of its life cycle?

# Designing the Alarm Circuit

*The building blocks of alarm circuits are very similar whatever situation they are being designed for. Basic circuits are joined together to produce the required function.*

## The Electronics

Alarm systems can be represented by a block diagram.

## Input Sensors

Depending on the type of alarm, you will need to identify the type of input which will set it off. For example, it could be light, heat or movement. The input will need a sensor which can detect the change you have identified. Pages 82-83 have details about a range of different sensors.

*A personal alarm with a range of input sensors*

## Sensitivity

The sensor will often need to be set at a particular sensitivity or range to work effectively. This is achieved by using the sensor in series with a variable resistor in an arrangement called a potential divider. Page 84 explains how potential dividers work.

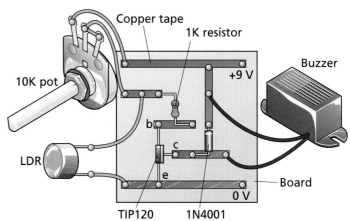

*A potential divider controlling a transistor switch*

## Enabling

A practical circuit will need to have a switch which activates the circuit. This is often called an 'enabling' or sometimes an 'arming' switch. Sensitive systems such as movement detectors will also need to have a time delay before they 'arm' themselves.

Pages 62-63 have ideas for circuits which have time delays.

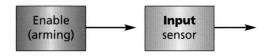

## Latching

If the alarm is triggered, i.e. something or someone sets it off, it will need to stay on until the user chooses to disarm it or switch it off. When a circuit stays in a certain state, i.e. the alarm stays on even though the input changes, we call this 'latching'.

Pages 86-88 have a number of ideas for latching circuits.

**■ ACTIVITY**

▶ Draw out the stages in the development of your alarm system as a series of blocks similar to the ones shown on the left.
▶ Using the circuits developed in this project, identify a possible solution to each of the blocks in your diagram.
▶ Identify the sensor, the output device and as many process building blocks as you can.

ALARMING CIRCUITS

system development

## Oscillating Circuits – Astables

If the output signal is going to be audible, like a buzzer or a siren, or visual such as a flashing LED or light, then it will usually require circuits which are oscillating, that is to say changing their state continually. These are called 'astable' circuits.

Pages 89-91 have a number of alternative astable circuits that will flash lights or provide pulses to a sound device.

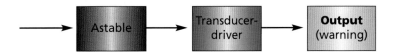

## Transducer-Drivers

The output will require enough power to drive it, so a transducer-driver circuit such as those found on pages 46-48 may be needed.

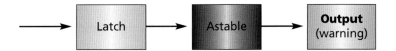

## Bigger Blocks

As the circuit for the product develops, so too will the block systems diagram.

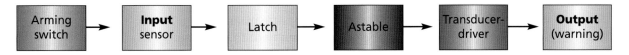

# Sensing

*The input to many control systems is often some sort of sensing device. These sensing devices are usually a mechanical switch, a transducer or a potential divider subsystem.*

## Mechanical Switches

Some common types of mechanical switches used as sensors are shown on the right.

Try to find out how these switches work. Can you name any other switches which might be used as sensors?

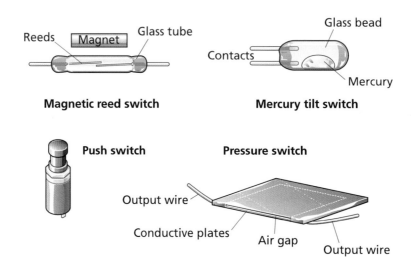

**Magnetic reed switch** — Reeds, Magnet, Glass tube

**Mercury tilt switch** — Glass bead, Contacts, Mercury

**Push switch**

**Pressure switch** — Output wire, Conductive plates, Air gap, Output wire

## Transducers

A transducer is a device which changes electrical energy into another form of energy, or vice versa. A microphone is an example of a transducer which is used as an input device. Some other examples of transducers are shown on page 46.

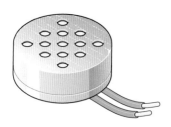

## Potential Divider Inputs

Many of the sensors you will use in building electronic devices use a change in resistance to control the circuit. An arrangement of two resistors in series with a power supply is called a potential divider. Page 84 has more details on potential dividers.

Common sensors used with this arrangement are the thermistor, the LDR (light-dependent resistor) and the moisture sensor.

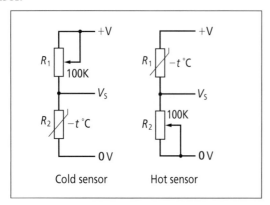

Cold sensor — $R_1$ 100K, $V_S$, $R_2$ $-t\,°C$, +V, 0V

Hot sensor — $R_1$ $-t\,°C$, $V_S$, $R_2$ 100K, +V, 0V

### Thermistors

A thermistor is a device whose resistance changes with temperature. You will probably use those whose resistance decreases as the temperature goes up. These are known as negative temperature coefficient thermistors.

Thermistors come in various forms: disc, rod and bead, and different sensitivity. You will probably use disc or bead thermistors. Thermistors are usually used in combination with fixed resistors or potentiometers as 'hot' or 'cold' sensors in a potential divider arrangement.

Bead

Disc

ORP12

**Symbol**

## Light-dependent resistors

A light-dependent resistor (LDR) is a device whose resistance changes with light level. The most common type of LDR is an ORP12, whose resistance decreases as the light level increases.

LDRs are usually used in combination with fixed resistors or potentiometers. They are used as 'light' or 'dark' sensors.

The resistance of an ORP12 changes from around 2 megohms in total dark to 100 ohms in bright light.

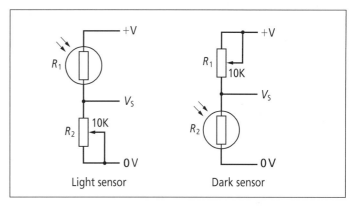

Light sensor                    Dark sensor

## Moisture sensors

Moisture sensors operate on the principle that water has less electrical resistance than air. They are high-impedance devices (i.e. they conduct little current) and simply consist of two conducting strips separated by a small air gap. If water bridges the gap the resistance of the sensor falls. They are usually used in series with high-value fixed resistors as potential divider inputs.

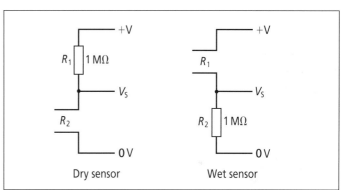

Dry sensor                    Wet sensor

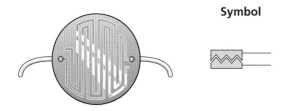

**Symbol**

Practical sensors often have the strips interleaved to increase their length for a given size of sensor. Why is this increase in length useful?

### ■ ACTIVITY

Make a list of possible uses for a moisture sensing circuit. Can you think of any problems you might have when making a product based around such circuits?

## Touch sensors

Touch sensors are very similar to moisture sensors. They also are made up of two conducting strips separated by an air gap, but this time the resistance decreases when skin bridges the gap. Touch sensors are often used on TVs for the channel buttons. They have the advantage of having no moving parts and therefore do not wear quickly. Touch sensor circuits are shown on pages 68–71.

# Potential Dividers

*Controlling the sensitivity of electronic sensors is the key to a successful product. Potential dividers are a way of adjusting the sensitivity of a circuit.*

## ■ ACTIVITY

Build a potential divider using a 10K and a 1K resistor arranged as shown in the diagram opposite.

► Connect the resistors to a 9V supply and then measure the voltage values at A and B using a multimeter.

► Try swapping the two resistors over. What happens to the voltage at B?

► Try two resistors with other values. Can you see a pattern?

Potential dividers are made from resistors connected in series between the +V and 0V supply lines of a circuit. They are used to control voltage levels and are commonly used in sensing circuits to control the sensitivity of the sensor. Thermistors, LDRs, moisture and touch sensors are usually used in a potential divider arrangement.

### How Potential Divider Inputs Control Circuits

Process circuits, such as transducer-drivers and logic gates, activate when supplied with a certain input voltage to the control connection ($V_s$). A simple example of this is the use of a transistor as a switch.

The base connection of a transistor switches on the transistor once the base voltage exceeds 0.6 V. If the transistor base is connected to a potential divider input, it can be made to act as an automatic switch triggered by heat, light, moisture, etc.

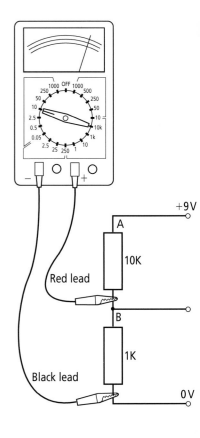

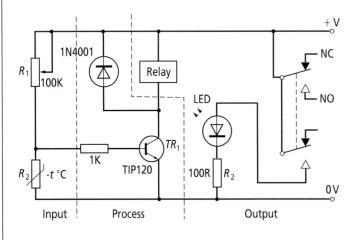

In the circuit for a temperature-controlled switch, $R_2$ is a thermistor and $R_1$ a variable resistor. In cool conditions most of the voltage is across $R_2$ and the transistor is on. As the temperature of the thermistor is raised the resistance falls and the voltage across $R_2$ falls. If it falls below 0.6 V the transistor switches off. This circuit could maintain the temperature at a steady level if the relay were used to switch a heater on and off.

## CALCULATIONS

The output voltage of a potential divider can be calculated by:

$$V_S = \frac{R_2}{R_1 + R_2} \times V$$

where
$V_S$ = output voltage,
$V$ = supply voltage,
$R_1$ and $R_2$ are resistance values.

e.g. If the supply voltage was 9V and $R_1$ and $R_2$ were 3K and 6K respectively, what would be the value of $V_S$?

$$V_S = \frac{6}{3+6} \times 9$$

$$= 6V$$

What would be the value of $V_S$ if $R_1$ were 6K and $R_2$ were 3K?

### KEY POINTS

- Potential dividers are made from two resistors in series with a power supply.
- The input to many electronic circuits is from a potential divider arrangement.
- Sensors such as thermistors and LDRs are used as part of a potential divider to control the sensitivity at which the switching action takes place.

## ■ ACTIVITY

Suppose you were designing a temperature warning device to tell a parent if a child's bedroom was getting too warm. Build the circuit which will light an LED if the room temperature is about 22°C. If you use a prototype board, it should look something like the one on the right. You will need to adjust the sensitivity of the potential divider to get it to switch at the correct temperature.

Adapt the potential divider to warn of the room being too cold, i.e. below 15°C.

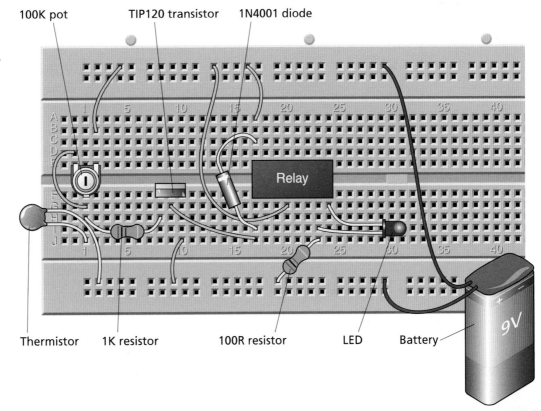

100K pot     TIP120 transistor     1N4001 diode

Thermistor     1K resistor     100R resistor     LED     Battery

# Bistables: Flip-Flops (1)

*Alarm systems which are triggered when someone breaks a light beam or treads on a pressure pad require an electronic building block which can store a temporary input signal. Bistables can latch, or hold, such temporary inputs.*

A bistable is a device which has two stable states. It can be made to change state by an input and will stay in that state until changed back to its original state by a second input. Bistables are also known as flip-flops and latches.

Mechanical switches can act as simple bistables, e.g. a push-to-make and push-to-break switch has two stable states. In a table lamp, pressing the switch turns the light on. It stays on until the switch is pressed again.

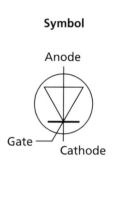

Symbol

Anode

Gate — Cathode

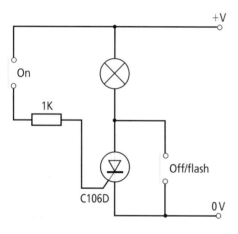

## Thyristors

A simple bistable latching circuit can be built using a thyristor. Thyristors are very similar in appearance to some transistors since they also have three legs. The legs are called the **anode**, the **cathode** and the **gate**.

When the thyristor is switched on it allows a current to flow through the anode and cathode. When it is off no current can flow.

The thyristor does not conduct until a positive voltage is applied to the gate, but once this has happened it latches 'on' even if the gate voltage is removed. The latch is removed by shorting across the anode and cathode.

### ■ ACTIVITY

► The circuit diagram shows a thyristor used in a simple light control circuit. Try building the circuit using self-adhesive copper tape for the connecting tracks, or on prototype board.
► If you use copper tape the circuit should look something like the one on the left.
► Try to explain how the circuit works – refer to the circuit diagram and the anode, cathode and gate in your explanation.

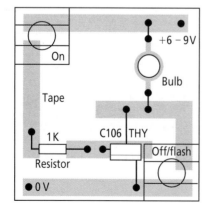

## Logic Gate/Feedback Flip-Flop

A bistable can be made using two NOT gates and a feedback resistor connected as shown in the diagram.

If the original state of the output is 'off' (logic 0) and the input to gate A is connected to a positive voltage value (logic 1), the output of A is 'off' (logic 0). If this is fed to the input of B the output flips to 'on' (logic 1). This logic 1 output is returned to the input via a resistor and this latches 'on' the output even if the original input is removed. Can you explain how the reset button works?

## A Practical Circuit

A practical version of this circuit can be made from a 4011 quad 2-input NAND gate IC. Inputs 1 and 2 are joined together to make the NAND gate act as a NOT gate, and the output, pin 3, is connected to both inputs of the second gate. Pin 4 is connected to both the output and the feedback resistor. The circuit latches 'on' once the input is taken 'high' and stays on until pins 1 and 2 are connected to 0 V via the reset button.

A 10K resistor is used as the feedback resistor. Why is the value of this resistor important?

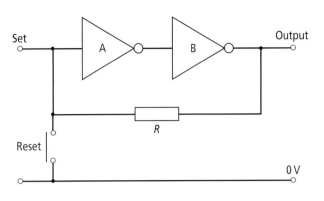

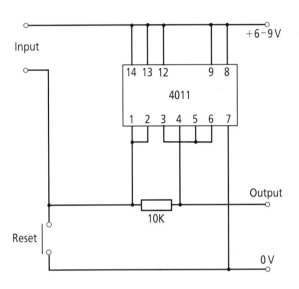

*Pin connections for a 4011 as a bistable*

*Bistables are the basic building blocks of computers. They 'remember' the last input*

■ **ACTIVITY**

This circuit is an example of the use of 'feedback' to control a digital circuit. Find out what this term means and other examples of the use of feedback in control.

See pages 42-43 for more information about logic gates.

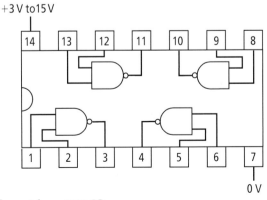

*Pin layout for a 4011 IC*

# Bistables: Flip-Flops (2)

ALARMING CIRCUITS

## A Schmitt Trigger Bistable

An improved version of the NOT gate flip-flop can be built using a 4093 IC. (This is a quad 2-input NAND Schmitt trigger chip and can be used to replace standard NAND gates.)

Using Schmitt gates improves the switching action when the input is 'noisy' or changing slowly.

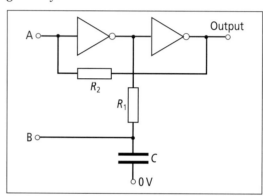

## How It Works

The output can be made to change between 'on' and 'off' by connecting the input to the junction of a resistor and capacitor series connected as shown in the diagram.

If input A is 'low' the output is also 'low'. The junction between the gates is 'high', however, and this charges the capacitor, $C$, via the resistor $R_1$. Connecting A to B now gives a 'high' to the input and so the output switches to 'high'. The feedback resistor, $R_2$, latches it in this state. This change of state makes the gate junction 'low' and so the capacitor discharges and B is now 'low'.

If A and B are now connected once more the input is taken 'low' and so the output switches 'off'. The output therefore changes state with alternate inputs.

The circuit will trigger with a high-impedance input and can be used as a touch switch where the input connection is made across the skin.

## Set-Reset Flip-Flop

A set-reset flip-flop is a type of bistable which responds well to electronic inputs. It has two inputs: set (S) and reset (R) which control two outputs, Q and Q̄. These two outputs latch in opposite states, as shown in the truth table.

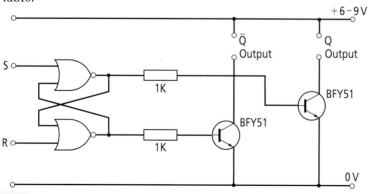

### IN YOUR PROJECT

Schmitt Trigger Bistables can be very useful in coursework projects, but will not be tested in the written examination.

### KEY POINTS

- Electronic bistable circuits can be used to store a temporary input signal by latching 'on' the output.
- Bistables can be made from thyristors and logic gates using feedback loops.
- Schmitt trigger NAND gates can cope better with inputs that are noisy or change gradually.

Truth table

| R | S | Q | Q̄ |
|---|---|---|---|
| 0 | 0 | No effect | |
| 0 | 1 | 0 | 1 |
| 1 | 0 | 1 | 0 |
| 1 | 1 | No effect | |

# Astables (1)

*Astables produce pulsed outputs. They are often used to control flashing lights and audible outputs. Astables can be used as the input to other circuits such as counters.*

An astable is a device which has no stable states. This means that when it is active it changes constantly from one state to another – on/off, high/low – until it runs out of energy.

A simple example of an astable device is a flashing bulb such as those used to control strings of fairy lights. Astables are also known as pulse generators and clocks.

### ■ ACTIVITY

Find out what is meant by a 'clocked input'.

## Pulse Generators

An electrical pulse is created when a device is turned on and then off again. The pulse could be thought of as a pulse of current or a pulse of voltage. If the device is turned on and off regularly, a train of pulses, or a signal, is produced.

The number of complete pulses produced per second is called the **frequency**. Frequency is measured in **hertz** (Hz).

The length of time taken for one pulse is called the **duration** of the pulse, $T$. The ratio of time on to time off for a pulse is known as the **mark/space ratio**.

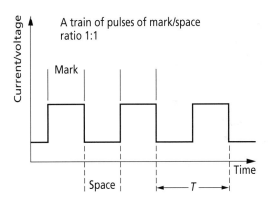

A train of pulses of mark/space ratio 1:1

## A 555 Timer Astable (with an equal mark/space ratio)

A 555 timer IC can be used to make an astable which will produce a chain of pulses. These can be used to make a sound, flash a light or switch on other building blocks such as bistable counters.

The 555 circuit shown on the left produces a mark/space ratio of 1:1, which means that it is off for the same length of time that it is on.

As with monstable circuits, the pulse frequency and duration depend upon the values of a resistor and capacitor.

The output is low powered and may need connecting to a transducer-driver to operate some output devices such as a loudspeaker.

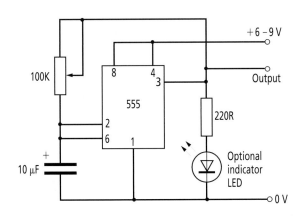

# Astables (2)

ICT

You could use a spreadsheet to design a simple frequency calculator.

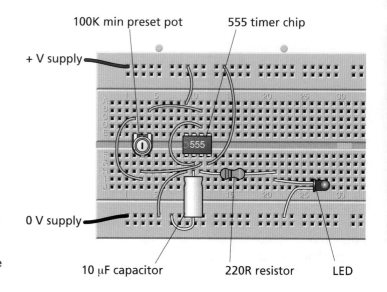

100K min preset pot     555 timer chip

+ V supply

0 V supply

10 µF capacitor          220R resistor          LED

## Building an Astable Circuit

Build the 555 timer IC astable shown on page 89 on a prototype board. It should look something like the one on the right when you have finished.

If you have connected up the components correctly the LED should flash on and off.

Try adjusting the potentiometer to see how it affects the LED output.

## A 555 Timer IC Astable (with an unequal mark/space ratio)

An astable with different on and off times can be useful in control circuits.

The on time (mark) depends upon $R_1$ and $C_1$, the off time (space) depends upon $R_2$ and $C_2$.

$T_1$ (mark) = $1.1 R_1 \times C_1$

$T_2$ (space) = $1.1 R_2 \times C_2$
(units = seconds)

The mark/space ratio for the circuit above would be approximately 1:2. Can you work out why?

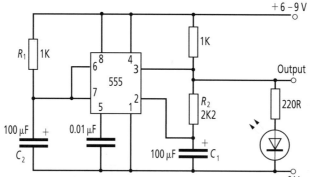

## Low Frequency/Long Pulse Duration

Astable circuits, like monostables, are controlled by charging and discharging capacitors. If high-value resistors and capacitors are used, the same problems of leakage as those described on page 67 occur. Astables with pulse duration of more than a few seconds are not therefore very reliable.

### ■ ACTIVITY

▶ Investigate the possible uses for astables of equal and unequal mark/space ratio outputs.

▶ Calculate the on and off times for an equal mark/space astable if $R$ is 100 k and $C$ is 100 µF.

---

The pulse frequency of the 555 astable output can be calculated using the equation:

$$\text{frequency } (f) = \frac{0.72}{R \times C} \text{ Hz}$$

e.g. a 1K resistor and a = 1 µF capacitor would produce pulses of frequency:

$$f = \frac{0.72}{1000 \times 1/1\,000\,000} = 720 \text{ Hz}$$

The pulse duration is given by:

$T = 1.4 R \times C$ (units = seconds)

## A Logic Gate Astable (equal mark/space ratio)

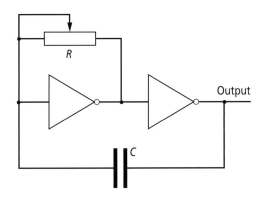

Two NOT gates used in combination with a potentiometer and a non-polarised capacitor can be used to make an astable with a mark/space ratio of 1:1 and variable frequency.

$R$ and $C$ control the pulse duration and frequency. $R$ could be a fixed resistor, but using a potentiometer gives you greater control and allows you to vary the frequency if required.

A practical version of this circuit could be built using a 4011 quad 2-input NAND gate IC connected to function as a NOT gate as shown.

Since $C$ is a non-polarised capacitor its value must be around $1\,\mu F$ or less. This means that $R$ must have a high value to give pulses suitable for many situations.

The output may need amplification via a transducer-driver to control some devices.

## A Logic Gate Astable (variable mark/space ratio)

The 4011 IC can also be used to make an astable with a variable mark/space ratio.

Find out why variable mark/space ratio astables are often used for motor speed control such as in electric drills.

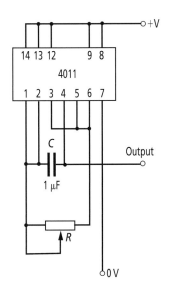

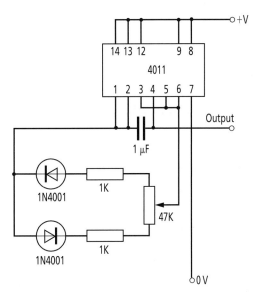

■ ACTIVITY

Build the circuit shown on the left on prototype board and use it to make an LED flash.

You will need to think carefully about how to connect the LED and what values of $R$ and $C$ to use to produce a flash rate of 2–4 hertz. The calculation on the previous page will help.

**KEY POINTS**

- Astables give pulsed outputs which constantly change from on to off.
- The 555 timer IC can be used to make astables. They are used as 'clocked inputs' to other circuits and for visual and audible outputs.
- The frequency and duration of the pulses depend upon the values of the control capacitor(s) and resistor(s).
- The mark/space ratio is the ratio of the time on to the time off.
- Astables can have equal or unequal mark/space ratios.
- Logic gates can be used to make astable circuits with both equal and unequal mark/space ratios.
- Astables with unequal mark/space ratios can be used in motor speed control circuits.
- The motor speed is controlled by pulsing the current running through it.

# Operational Amplifiers

*Operational amplifiers (op-amps) have many uses but you are most likely to use them as either an electronic switch or a voltage amplifier. Op-amps have a number of advantages over transistors as amplifiers – they are more reliable and efficient and draw less current from the power supply.*

Operational amplifiers have two inputs and one output and are commonly made as DIL (dual-in-line) integrated circuits. A common type is a 741 op-amp which is an 8-pin chip. The two inputs are called the inverting and the non-inverting inputs.

**IN YOUR PROJECT**

If you need a circuit which can detect small changes in a sensor input, then an op-amp is a useful building block.

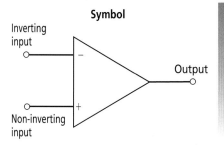

Symbol

## The Op-Amp as a Comparator

Op-amps can be used as digital electronic switches.

If both inputs are used, the op-amp compares the inverting input voltage with the non-inverting input voltage and gives a 'high' or 'low' output depending upon which is greater.

If the non-inverting input is higher the output is 'high', and if the inverting input is higher the output is 'low'.

This type of circuit is known as a **comparator** and it is able to detect very small changes at the inputs.

741 and 3140 op-amps

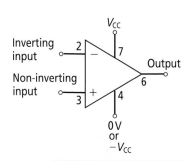

### ■ ACTIVITY

▶ The circuit diagram shows an op-amp used as a moisture-activated comparator.

▶ Can you explain how the circuit works? Which LED would be lit if the sensor were dry?

▶ Try building the circuit on prototype board to check whether you are right.

▶ Describe a practical use for this circuit.

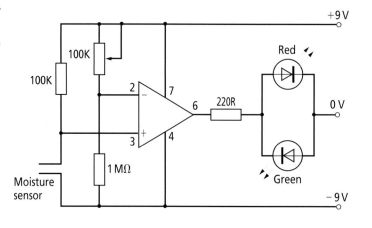

**KEY POINTS**

● Op-amps are used as comparators and voltage amplifiers. They have two inputs – inverting and non-inverting.

● Comparators are controlled by comparing voltages at the two inputs.

● An inverting amplifier gives an output of opposite polarity to the input. gain = $-R_f/R_{in}$.

The gain is controlled by negative feedback.

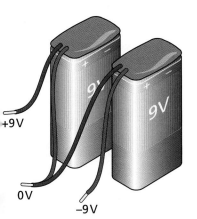

+9V
0V
−9V

*electronic components*

## Using an Op-Amp IC

3140 and 741 op-amp ICs work best with pins 4 and 7 connected to − 9V and + 9V respectively.

This can be achieved by joining two 9V (PP3) batteries in series and connecting them to the circuit as shown.

### 741 or 3140?

The 3140 op-amp IC is very similar to the 741 but has the advantage of working with a lower voltage supply. The 741 needs ± 5 V or more whereas the 3140 will work down to ± 2 V.

## The Op-Amp as a Voltage Amplifier

Operational amplifiers are also commonly used as voltage amplifiers. They are most often used as inverting amplifiers. This means that the output has the opposite polarity to the input. A positive input gives negative output and vice versa.

## Voltage Gain

The gain of the amplifier is controlled by the input resistor ($R_{in}$) and the feedback resistor ($R_f$). The feedback resistor is used to take part of the output back to the input. This is known as **negative feedback** and has the advantages of making the amplifier more stable and the gain more predictable.

$$\text{gain} = \frac{V_{out}}{V_{in}} = \frac{-R_f}{R_{in}}$$

If $R_f$ was 100K and $R_{in}$ 1K the gain would be 100. The minus sign shows that it is an inverting amplifier.

## An Infrared Remote-Controlled Switch

The circuit diagram shows a 3140 op-amp used to amplify the input signal from an infrared sensor as part of a remote-controlled switch.

The signal from the transmitter is pulsed to save energy. This means that the output from the amplifier is also pulsed. The demodulator is needed to smooth out this output before it is fed to the transistor base.

Find out more about modulation and demodulation.

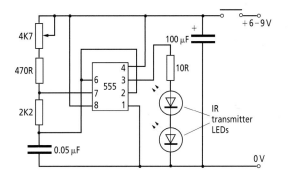

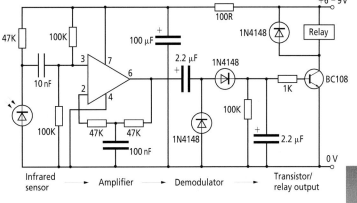

Infrared sensor → Amplifier → Demodulator → Transistor/relay output

*The IR transmitter is pulsed using an astable*

### IN YOUR PROJECT

Would an infrared detector be useful in your design? It could be used to switch a device on and off without touching it.

# Power Supplies

*Once a customer has purchased an electronic product they will have the additional running cost of the power supply. The specification of the voltage, size and capacity of the power supply is an essential design consideration.*

*A a digital joulemeter can help you find the energy consumption of your circuit*

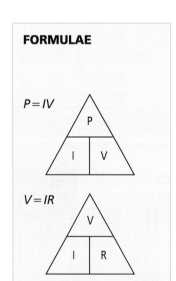

## Electrical Energy

Scientists now use the **joule** as the unit in which energy is measured. To give you some idea of the size of a joule, it takes about 400 000 joules of energy to boil a kettle of water. When transferring this amount of energy it's cheaper to use a mains supply rather than a battery.

Most electronic circuits transfer much smaller quantities of energy. In most cases this will only be a few joules, so the limited amount of energy stored in the chemicals of a cell or battery will operate most electronic devices hundreds of times.

### FORMULAE

$P = IV$

$V = IR$

If you learn these 'magic triangles' they can help you rearrange formulae to find the value of any variable if you know the other two, for example

$$I = \frac{P}{V} \quad \text{or} \quad I = \frac{V}{R}.$$

## ■ ACTIVITY

Suppose you have an LED in your circuit which must only carry a maximum current of 50 mA and is made to operate at 2.5 V. Calculate:
▶ the power it transfers to heat and light;
▶ the effective resistance.

## Power Calculations

Sometimes it is useful to measure the **power** of an electrical supply. Power is a measure of the energy used each second, i.e. joules per second.

1 joule delivered each second (1 J/s) is called 1 **watt**.

watts = joules/seconds

Power is also important when calculating how much thermal energy is transferred when a current passes through a component.

Power can be calculated from the equation:

$P = IV$

where $P$ = power (in watts), $I$ = current (in amps), $V$ = voltage (in volts).

If you can measure the current flowing in a circuit and the voltage supplied, you can calculate the power.

Most electronic components have a power rating. When designing, you should not exceed the power rating in case the component overheats. A typical power rating for a carbon film resistor would be 0.25 W.

Find the maximum safe current for a 10K resistor by combining the formula for resistance with the formula for calculating power.

## Cell Capacity

The capacity of cells to deliver electric current is often measured in ampere hours (A h).

Multiplying the current (in amperes) by the time is a measure of the amount of charge which the cell can deliver to a circuit.

The specified discharge time is usually 8 hours. A battery with a rating of 20 A h would therefore be able to provide $20/8 = 2.5$ A for 8 hours, or less current for a proportionately longer time.

## Value For Money

Making a value-for-money comparison between different cells is difficult. This is because the amount of time a cell or battery can deliver a particular current or voltage depends on a number of factors such as:

▷ age of the cell/battery;
▷ design and quality of manufacture;
▷ physical size;
▷ number of times each day it is used;
▷ temperature;
▷ current delivered with each operation.

Generally, costs increase as shown in the table on page 37. Button cells are a very expensive way of buying electricity but their size makes them very important in some applications such as watches and hearing aids. Rechargeable cells and batteries are initially expensive to purchase but can work out much cheaper over a period of time.

For miniaturised circuits with low current consumption, such as a timer, it may be possible to use a mercury oxide button cell, but if the circuit needs to drive a transducer such as a solenoid or even to light standard LEDs for any length of time then something the size of at least an AA cell is required.

## Cell Holders and Connectors

Most circuits contain components which need between 3 V and 12 V to operate them. You will therefore need to mount a number of cells in series to create the required voltage. There are a variety of holders to choose from. Look at the dimensions and the voltage you require before you decide on the right one.

How will the customer get access to replace the battery or cells?

# Finalising the Circuit

*Once you have decided on the electronic building blocks you require to build your alarm circuit, you can move on to joining them together.*

## Schematic Diagrams

For a cycle alarm the circuit block diagram could look like the one below.

The input sensor could be a mercury tilt or a trembler switch which will detect movement.

You should then be able to sketch out a schematic diagram similar to the one below. Pages 86-90 provide details of the building blocks you might use such as astables and latches.

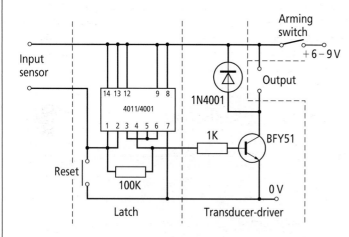

Collect together the components you will need. Check the values of resistors and capacitors carefully. Then make up the temporary circuit on a prototype board.

If your design appears to work well then you should draw the schematic diagram neatly and label it.

It is a good idea to try and draw in where each part of the circuit fits the block diagram.

Lay out the components and decide on how much space you need. Remember – the circuit board will need to fit inside the casing you design.

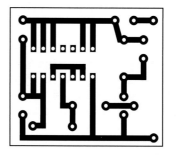 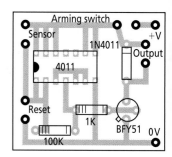

*Possible PCB and component layout*

Once you have a component layout you can move to designing the tracks joining the components. This may take a number of attempts to avoid crossing tracks. Remember that computer-aided design (CAD) can be useful in PCB design.

Page 133 shows how to make a PCB using the photo-resist method.

## Evaluating the Electronics

How could your design be developed and improved?

▷ Have you considered having a time delay before the alarm sounds? Pages 62-64 have circuits for time delays.
▷ Could the arming switch be a key for security? It could be a digital combination code.

There are many possible developments, all of which you will need to balance against the customers' responses and the effect on the selling price.

# Designing the Container

▷ *What shapes will look good and do the job?*
▷ *What size should it be?*
▷ *What will be the largest component that has to be contained?*
▷ *How will the power supply be replaced?*
▷ *How will unauthorised people be prevented from having access to the electronics?*

## Designing Through Modelling

Drawings help you work out and record ideas quickly. As designers begin to develop their proposals in more detail, they use 3D models and mock-ups to check out how well they look and work.

Models, mock-ups and prototypes have the advantage of helping you see your ideas in 3D. They enable you to look at your designs from different angles – sometimes designs that look promising on paper don't work in reality.

You can also use 3D models to check that all the components will fit into the product, and to help you arrange them in the best position. Can you get to the battery easily to change it? How easy will it be to assemble the components?

Finally, you can check your ideas in the situation in which they are designed to operate. For example, products that are designed to be hand-held, such as torches, hair dryers and travel games, need to be comfortable to hold. Only by actually holding the product will you be able to test this properly. Another example might be products that need to fit inside a pocket – a block model will allow you to check this.

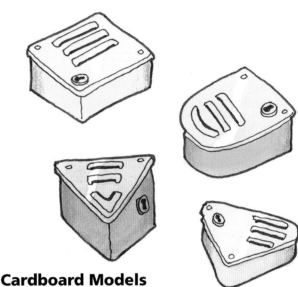

## Cardboard Models

Card is one of the quickest ways of making an early mock-up to check sizes and internal layouts.

## Block Models

If you need to check your design in more detail, you might decide a block model is more appropriate. Using a solid block of rigid foam is quick and easy, but you need to control the waste material – it is dangerous to inhale the dust. An alternative might be softwood or MDF. Block modelling also has the advantage of allowing you to try out more complex and sculptural shapes.

Start with a block exactly the size of the final product. Carefully mark out and cut away shapes, finally adding any rounded edges. This is known as a 'wasting process'.

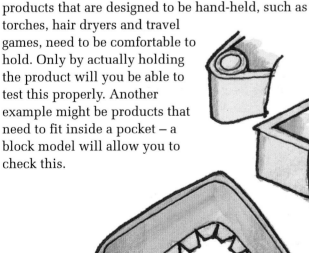

### ■ ACTIVITY

Draw out some initial ideas for the product which show the layout of the electronic components, power supply, etc.

Pages 120-125 offer advice on product modelling techniques and the use of other materials that this project may require.

# Designing the Inside of Products

*The design of the inside of your product casing needs as much thought as its outside. All the components must be fit it and be held firmly in the correct place.*

You could use CAD software to ensure all the parts will fit into your case.

When you are arranging the layout for the components, consider whether there is a right or wrong place for each item:

▷ Should certain items be near each other?
▷ Does the battery need a separate compartment?

The position of some components will be governed by the outside appearance.

You might well want to keep the product as small as you can. Electronic products can be reduced in size by eliminating all wasted space inside the product. Smaller products are also cheaper to manufacture.

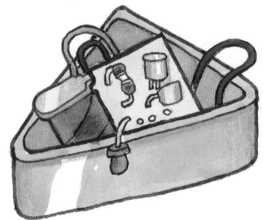

*Avoid a jumble...*

## Adding Internal Detail

When approaching the detail design, product designers try and build features into the plastic casing. If they can mould a detail into the plastic which will hold the pcb then that will save the cost of extra components and another assembly process.

## Inside Access

You will need to consider how to get inside your product, both for initial assembly and for 'after-sales care', should the product stop working. You will also need to change the battery from time to time.

Using removable countersunk screws is one simple method that can be used:

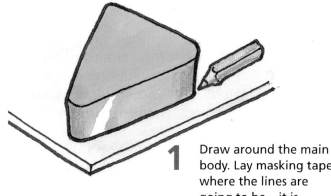

**1** Draw around the main body. Lay masking tape where the lines are going to be – it is easier to see the marks.

**2** Glue strips of plastic in the main case. The strips should fit in place snuggly with minimum gaps.

**3** Hold the lid in place with masking tape and drill the holes. The hole diameter should match the core diameter of the self-tapping screws that will be used. Make sure they are marked out accurately – it is important that they are central with the strips beneath and also look neat.

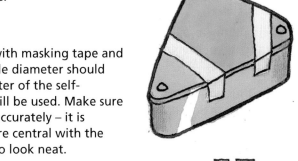

**4** The holes in the lid will need to be drilled out to clearance size and countersunk.

---

### Different solutions

**1.** This solution has the lid set in. It looks neater but it is more difficult to construct. Make the lid at the same time as the base of the main body, for greater accuracy.

**2.** This idea is useful for vacuum-formed product models where you wish to retain the flange. It avoids the screw threads being seen.

**3.** This design has a clip at one end and two screw fixings at the other.

**4.** This idea has a positive location for the cover.

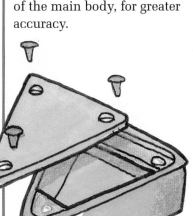

# Planning and Making Final Product Models (1)

*It is important that you aim to make your product realisation as accurately as you can. The quality of your product will be assessed in terms of precision and finish, regardless of how ambitious your project is. Remember this applies to the electronics as well as the product casing. You might consider vacuum forming for the casing.*

## Planning the Making

Make sure you have final drawings of your circuit and container. The drawings should show clearly the sizes and shapes of the container.

Prepare a list of all the different materials and making stages you will need. Estimate how long each main stage will take.

▷ What operations could be going on at the same time? Draw a flow chart to illustrate what you will need to do and when.
▷ How and when will you be checking the accuracy of your making?
▷ What specific safety precautions will you need to observe during the making process?

## Making a Rectangular Box

When marking out, use an engineer's square to guarantee that things are cut and assembled at right angles. When measuring, always work to within a small tolerance, e.g. + or −0.5 mm. (See page 136 for more about working to tolerance.)

If you mark out and cut very carefully you should be able to avoid sanding. If necessary, a jig will help you sand edges and ends accurately.

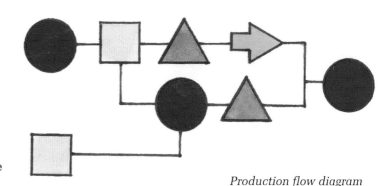

*Production flow diagram*

The best way to make a box is to calculate the overall length of all four sides and cut one long strip. You can then cut the sides to length, but remember the lengths of the sides will not necessarily be the same as the outside dimensions of the box.

When you are assembling, check that the sides are at right angles to each other. Also ensure the diagonals are the same.

It is often easier to add details such as holes etc. before assembly. This is all part of the planning you need to do in advance.

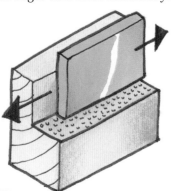

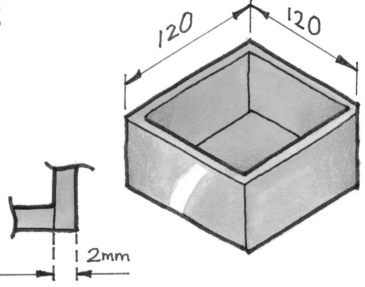

## Making a Moulded Box Using a Vacuum Former

To make a mould which can be used in a vacuum former bond two blocks of MDF together using double-sided tape. Glue a photocopied drawing of the shape onto the surface. Cut the shape out using a band saw and sand carefully to the line.

Prize the two halves apart and use a sander to add a draft angle. Carefully sand a radius on the appropriate edges.

Page 122 has more details on vacuum formers.

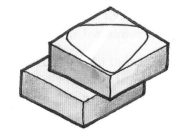
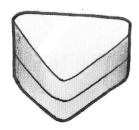

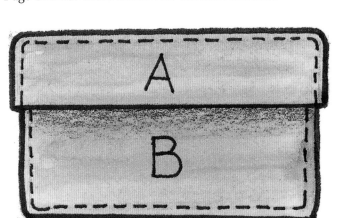

You could make the two halves of the casing different depths.

Moulding A will be thicker at the 'shut line' than moulding B. This is because the plastic on mould B will have thinned more, having been drawn down further. One solution is to use different thickness plastic sheet for each moulding.

Remember that the mould must be approximately 6–8 mm deeper than the finished moulding to allow for trimming the plastic.

## Locating the Lid

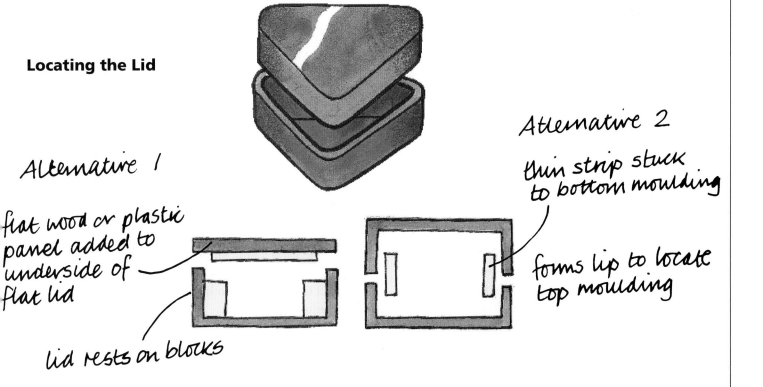

Alternative 1

flat wood or plastic panel added to underside of flat lid

lid rests on blocks

Alternative 2

thin strip stuck to bottom moulding

forms lip to locate top moulding

# Planning and Making Final Product Models (2)

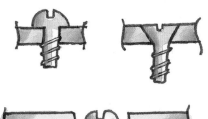

## HOLDING A COVER IN PLACE

*The finish of a product model is important if the client is to get a sound idea of the finished product – small details are vital.*

▷ *Mark out accurately the centres for the screw holes on the cover.*
▷ *Fit the lid to the main case with the battery holder bonded into place.*
▷ *Drill pilot holes through the cover and the battery holder.*
▷ *Tap these holes with a suitable thread to match the chosen screw size.*

## Improving the Appearance

▷ Use dome-headed screws.
▷ Recess the screw heads screws.
▷ Make plastic washers using a plug cutter and bond them to the underside of the cover.
▷ Add clearance holes. A strip of plastic could be used instead. An alternative solution would be countersunk screws.

## Feature Details

Cover detailing over speakers and buzzers can be difficult and unsightly. Here are two methods you might use or adapt.

The first approach is to use pierced holes. This gives you a matrix of holes perfectly spaced.

Use matrix board which is normally used for prototyping circuits and attach it to the area that requires piercing.

▷ Carefully mark out the area that requires the holes and, using a pcb drill, drill through the matrix board and plastic.
▷ Plan to drill in rows rather than at random – it is easy to miss a hole and you will not find out until you remove the matrix board!
▷ Drill the holes methodically using a small drill. 1.5 mm is a good size.
▷ It is important to ensure that the plastic does not build up on the drill. This will melt and make unsightly holes.

Alternatively, use a speaker fabric grill and a plastic collar. You will need a piece of plastic tube from which to cut a collar approximately 8 mm long (plastic overflow pipe is about the right size) and speaker fabric or a fabric that will stretch.

▷ Drill a hole fractionally larger than the plastic tube.
▷ Stretch the fabric over the tube and press the tube carefully into the hole from the inside. A few drops of superglue will secure it in place. The grill can be flush or raised.

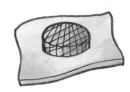

## Finishing Your Product

The final coat of paint will only be as good as the surface it is put on. Only paint your product when all the making has been completed. Assemble the product completely and check that you are satisfied with it. Carefully remove all components and prepare the product for spraying.

The plastic should be smooth and all blemishes eliminated. Using silicon carbide paper, starting perhaps with 240 grade, work carefully on the surfaces using a sanding block. Use progressively finer grades, ending up with 600 grade, until you have eliminated all blemishes.

You may wish to radius edges. This requires great care and concentration. Make sure you don't go too far, taking care to keep an even radius on all edges.

## Painting

It is important to use a primer and avoid using different types of paints – cellulose and acrylic paints can react with each other and act like paint stripper! If in doubt, check on a scrap piece of plastic.

A number of light coats is better than one heavy one that might cause unsightly runs and sags.

The paint will be touch dry in a few minutes. Don't be tempted to start assembling the product at once. Leave it at least overnight, preferably for a few days.

## Spray Paints

When spraying you should use a well-ventilated area with a suitable extraction system. Stand the various pieces of the casing separately on blocks of wood or hang them from pieces of wire. Try and choose a size of block that allows the product to overhang or the paint will stick the product to the block.

Arrange the pieces so that they can be rotated. Spray lightly. Start the spray off the object and continue the spray slightly past it. Avoid using circular motions.

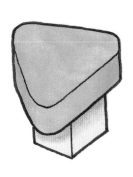
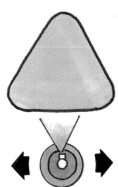

If your product model is vacuum formed and you are careful, you can avoid painting the plastic by taking advantage of its mirror finish.

WWW. To find out more about toys and games currently on the market, go to: www.tru.com

**IN YOUR PROJECT**
▶ Plan the making of the casing and electronic components carefully.
▶ Work as accurately as you can: precision and quality of finish are essential.

# Presenting to a Client / Testing and Evaluation

*How are you going to convince Acme Alarms that your design ideas are good enough for them to invest hundreds of thousands of pounds in setting up a production line, promotional materials and a distribution network?*

*What evidence have you got that your ideas will work?*

## Planning the Presentation

What exactly have Acme Alarms asked you to develop for them? Keep this firmly in mind as you plan your presentation. It might be a good idea to prepare a series of display panels to help show:

▷ who the product is aimed at;
▷ the situations in which it might be used;
▷ how it differs from other existing solutions;
▷ the main electronic building blocks and components;
▷ how the casing fits together, and how the electronics fit inside.

You will also need a number of technical drawings of circuit diagrams and orthographic drawings of the casing.

Taking your product model to show them would obviously be a good idea, along with a technical report. This would provide details of technical specifications, test results, component quantities and anticipated production costs. Where possible, illustrate this material with diagrams, charts and graphs.

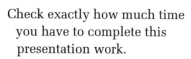

Check exactly how much time you have to complete this presentation work.

▷ How will you divide your time up?
▷ What are the priorities?

Prepare a plan of action. Keep a diary record of how things go, noting the changes you needed to make as you went along.

## Testing the Presentation

Show your work to some people who have not seen your ideas before. Identify some key questions to ask them to discover how well they understand your ideas. For example:

▷ What sort of people is the alarm aimed at?
▷ What words would you use to describe its shape, colours and graphic details?
▷ Can you tell what the controls and displays do?
▷ What are its key design features?

As you ask these questions, try and notice which display panels the viewer is looking at to find the answers.

▷ Which drawings provide the most helpful information?
▷ What information is missing?

Also invite open comments and questions.

*final realisation*

## Testing the Alarm

▷ How easy is it to activate and deactivate? How easy is it for the wrong person to deactivate the alarm?

▷ Does it go off too easily at the wrong time? Does this mean you need a time delay?

▷ Is the fixing secure, i.e. can the alarm be ripped off? What tools would a person need to remove it carefully?

▷ Is the warning too loud or too faint?

▷ Have you indicated the type of cell or battery customers must use? Is this shown clearly on the product?

▷ Will the electronics be damaged by connecting the power supply the wrong way round? Can this be prevented in the design of the circuit or the type of connector used?

▷ Can you change the battery without dismantling the whole container?

▷ Is the electronic circuit fastened inside securely?

What other tests can you devise?

▷ Is it strong enough to withstand normal knocks? Set up a 'fair test' that is not destructive. Perhaps you could hit the case with a fixed force a number of times. Record the results.

▷ Is it waterproof? Test the container using a water spray (without the electronics if necessary). Dry off the outside and then examine the inside for water. Cobalt chloride paper from the science department can be used to test for moisture (turning from blue to pink).

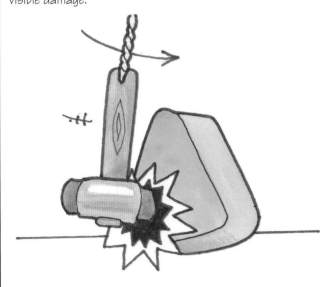

### Test Methods and Results

I used a rubber hammer as a pendulum and struck the casing with a force of 50 newtons, 100 times without any visible damage.

*You will need to show how your product fits onto the bicycle*

## Final Evaluation

While evaluating your container design consider ergonomics, durability and visual appeal in particular.

Evaluate the alarm in its normal environment. Use it yourself and, even better, get someone else to try it out. Provide them with a report form to fill in at the end of, say, a week. This will need to be easy for them to complete.

Show the alarm to people who may use it. Get just an instant response:

▷ Do they know what it is?
▷ Have they felt the need for this type of alarm?
▷ Do they like the look of it?
▷ Suggest some possible selling prices. How much would they be prepared to pay?

Look back at your original design proposal. Use the criteria as a checklist and comment on the extent to which the final product meets the original specification.

Refer directly to your final evaluation when discussing the successes and failures of your work.

Remember also to write in detail about the design development process you went through.

# Examination Questions

*You should spend about one and a half hours answering the following questions. To complete the paper you will need some A4 and plain A3 paper, basic drawing equipment, and colouring materials. You are reminded of the need for good English and clear presentation in your answers.*

**1.** **This question is about sensing.**
*(Total 17 marks)* See pages 92-93.

A sports company wants to design a device to accurately sense when the light level drops below a certain point. A green LED must come on when it is bright and a red LED must come on when it is dark. The circuit for this is shown below.

a)    What sensing component would you use to sense light?
*(1 mark)*

b)    The input part of many systems is called a potential divider. Draw a potential divider and explain how it works. *(5 marks)*

c)    Transducers can be used as an input component. Explain how a transducer is different from a mechanical switch. *(2 marks)*

d)    The company has decided to use an operational amplifier in the final circuit. This is shown below. Explain how the level of light needed to switch the green LED on can be adjusted. *(2 marks)*

e)    Explain how the op-Amp. Uses the voltages at pins 2 & 3 to control the output voltage. *(4 marks)*

f)    The red LED is missing from the circuit diagram. Add the component and explain your reasons for your answer. *(3 marks)*

**2.** **This question is about Bistables.** *(Total 12 marks)* See pages 86-88.

a)    Describe the operation of a bistable. Explain why are they used in alarm systems. *(4 marks)*

b)    A thyristor can be used in a bistable. What are the names of its three legs and describe its operation? *(5 marks)*

c)    Explain how a bistable can be made by using logic. *(3 marks)*

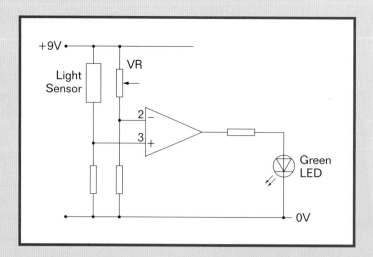

## 3. This question is about timing.

*(Total 11 marks)* See pages 89-91.

When it becomes too dark the company wants to add an audible warning. They have decided to use an astable circuit to do this. This is shown on the right.

a)  What do you understand by the term astable? *(1 mark)*

b)  What function does R1 and C1 perform? *(2 marks)*

c)  The buzzer does not work very well. Improve the circuit diagram so the buzzer gives a clear sound. *(3 marks)*

d)  The company wants to further develop the circuit so the alarm comes on for a set period of time. What type of timing circuit would you use to perform this function? *(1 mark)*

e)  Draw the final system diagram for the circuit. *(4 marks)*

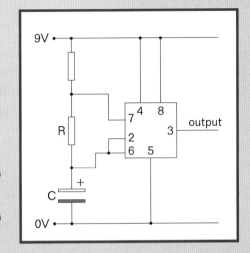

## 4. This question is about manufacturing in plastic and casing design. *(Total 20 marks)*
See pages 97-105.

a)  The circuit will need to be housed in a pocket-sized case. Draw a design for this. Explain the materials you would use if you were to make 10 prototypes in a school workshop. *(6 marks)*

b)  How would you change the design and manufacturing process if the company were to make 10,000 of the case? Explain what material you would use. *(5 marks)*

c)  Once you have completed the manufacture of the prototypes explain how you would check to find out if the design is suitable for its intended use. *(3 marks)*

d)  Explain how Computer Aided Design (CAD) could be used in the design and construction of the case. *(3 marks)*

e)  Draw a flow diagram to explain how circuit board would be made and assembled. *(3 marks)*

**Total marks = 60**

# Project Four: Introduction

*Inexpensive electronic components, mass production techniques and miniaturisation have made it possible to design products which, only a few years ago, would have been unacceptably expensive or even impossible to manufacture.*

## Design Brief

You and some close friends want to form a new electronic production company. The idea is to use your knowledge and experience to add electronics to conventional toys and games.

The UK market for toys and games is worth many millions of pounds. A new twist to an established product can often restore falling or static sales.

## The Task

In order to convince someone to provide the necessary financial backing you need to develop one idea to the point of small batch production. This will help establish the commercial potential of your design.

## First Thoughts

### Mix and match

At a more educational level, a simple 'matching pairs' game can be made more appealing with a variety of sounds and flashing lights.

### Listening books

Electronics also adds new ideas to books. Sound-making circuits can now be made small enough to fit in the pages of a book.

### Light and sound

A simple car or a toy telephone can be transformed by adding light or sounds.

## ■ ACTIVITY

▶ Decide on an existing toy or game which you feel has potential to develop its sales through adding electronics.

▶ Produce annotated sketches of some of your first ideas.

▶ Show them to some children, some parents, even a toy shop.

▶ What reactions do you get? Try to estimate the retail cost and test people's reaction to the anticipated price.

▶ Make sure you record your findings.

### On the move

Movement in toys always attracts attention. Small inexpensive motors can be driven from electronic circuits.

### Time's up!

A set time for each player's turn can add excitement and give a game more pace.

## Market Research

Market researchers and designers often test and evaluate existing products in order to identify ways in which designs might be improved in terms of manufacture, performance and sales potential.

A company's product may be systematically tested using a variety of information and data-gathering techniques, and its performance compared with its competitors' products. Its maintenance and method of manufacture may be analysed to determine potential modifications.

## Evaluating the Competition

What similar sorts of products are already available? Try to obtain some to examine. If necessary, viewing them on display in a shop will give you useful information on:

▷ price
▷ target age range
▷ colour
▷ texture
▷ weight
▷ visual appeal.

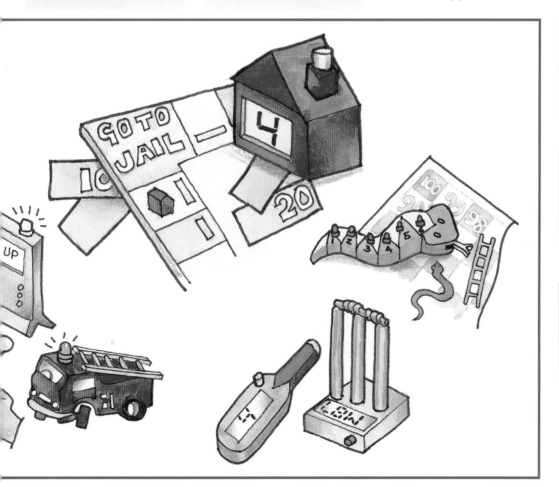

### Keeping count

Scoring can also be done electronically. Pressing a button, or creating a signal made from a contact during the game, can use a counter to keep a record.

### Steady hands

Co-ordination games can be made more exciting if mistakes result in a variety of effects made possible by electronics.

### Throwing a six to start

Many games use a dice to add the element of chance to the game. Electronics can offer an alternative way of providing a number.

# Project Development/Specification

*The stages in developing the idea of an electronic dice are presented here.*

*If you follow a similar approach when designing most electronic products, you will produce an effective design proposal.*

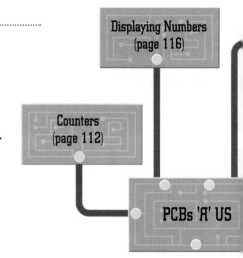

Displaying Numbers (page 116)

Counters (page 112)

PCBs 'Я' US

## Product Specification

Traditional dice-based games work on moves that are from 1 to 6, i.e. the six sides of a cube. Electronic dice could allow moves of 10 or more, and 0 is also an option not available on a cube. What opportunities does this offer for developing existing games?

▷ Will the 'dice' be passed around from player to player, or will it be mounted as a feature of the game board?

▷ Will the result of the 'roll' be as visible to all players as a normal cube dice? Is this an important element in anticipation?

▷ Would a sound be useful to add to the effect of a 'roll', e.g. a sound which changes frequency before the result is displayed?

▷ Will there still be the element of randomness associated with rolling a cube dice?

▷ Should the 'roll' of the electronic dice be initiated by pressing a button?

▷ What range of numbers will you need to display? An LED or a lamp could be set against an array of numbers. Would it be better to have an electronic number such as those shown on a watch or calculator?

The answers to these questions should form the basis of your product specification. There will still be many further design issues to be resolved and included. Pages 20-21 have information on these.

### Specification

✔ The die should show numbers from 1 to 9.

✔ The number should be visible from two meters.

✔ The switch should be flush with the surface of the die.

✔ A 'beep' should sound for two seconds when the switch is pressed.

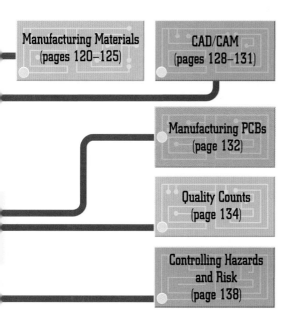

## Developing the Electronics

Your circuit could be developed from a range of different counters and types of display. A counter which outputs to a visual display might contain the following units:

▷ A clock input to drive the counter. This could be an astable such as the ones discussed on pages 89-91.
▷ A counter circuit started and stopped by the player using the 'enable' connection.
▷ An LED/seven-segment display.

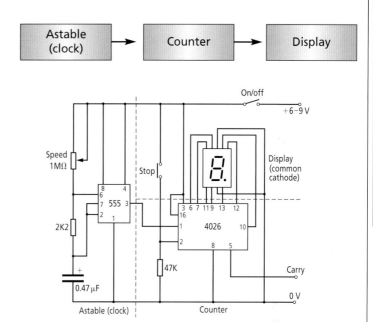

## Counting the Pulses

The pulses from the astable would be counted using some sort of binary or decade counter circuit. Counters are discussed on pages 112-113.

## Displaying the Count

LEDs are commonly used as indicators for counting circuits. These can be arranged to give a binary or decimal readout, though most people would only understand a decimal figure. Seven-segment displays are a way of using the output from a counting circuit to make shapes which look like decimal numbers.

## Controlling the Count

Counter circuits can be made to start and stop counting using the 'enable' connection. Visually the count is started if the enable is connected to 'low' and stopped if it is taken to 'high'.

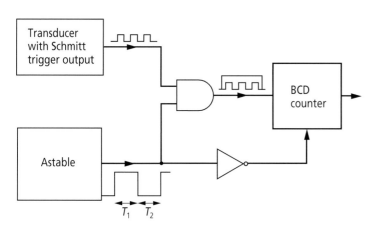

### IN YOUR PROJECT

► Develop a product specification for your toy/game.
► Represent the electronics using a systems diagram.

PCBs 'Я' US

*project development*

# Counters

*If you need to:*
▷ **count a number of events, such as the number of times a button is pressed;**
▷ **make a light flash a set number of times;**
▷ **flash a sequence of lights;**
▷ **show numbers using a seven-segment display**
*then you will require a counting circuit.*

Electronic counting circuits are used in a variety of products such as digital watches, event counters and timers used in audio and video recorders, and electronic dice. They can store each input they receive. The number of counts is usually shown by lighting a series of LEDs or an LCD (liquid crystal display).

The count is commonly triggered by an input pulse from an astable circuit, a sensing circuit or a mechanical switch.

It is important that the input pulse is clean or the counter might change by more than one for each pulse. Cleaning the input pulse is often called **debouncing**.

## A Debouncing Circuit: a Schmitt Trigger

A Schmitt trigger is a type of bistable whose output changes very rapidly from one state to the other. Schmitt triggers are commonly used to produce clean inputs for counting circuits.

You will probably find them most useful for debouncing switches and changing the output from analogue sensors, such as LDRs and thermistors, into digital signals.

They can be made in a number of ways. One way is to use specially made ICs such as the 40106 which has six Schmitt trigger inverters.

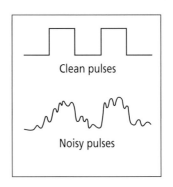

Clean pulses

Noisy pulses

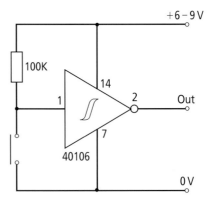

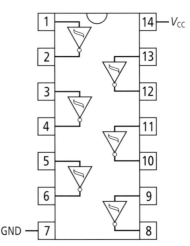

112

# Decade Counter

The 4017 decade counter IC can be used to drive a series of LEDs as a ten event counter if connected as shown in the diagram.

The counter advances one count on each 'low' to 'high' pulse provided to pin 14 (clock input) and light the LEDs in turn.

The counter is reset by taking pin 15 'high' momentarily, and stopped by taking pin 13 (enable) 'high'.

The output of pin 15 is 'high' for the first five input pulses and 'low' for the next five. This is called a 'divide by ten' function since the output frequency is one-tenth of the input frequency.

The output here can be fed to another counter or indicator.

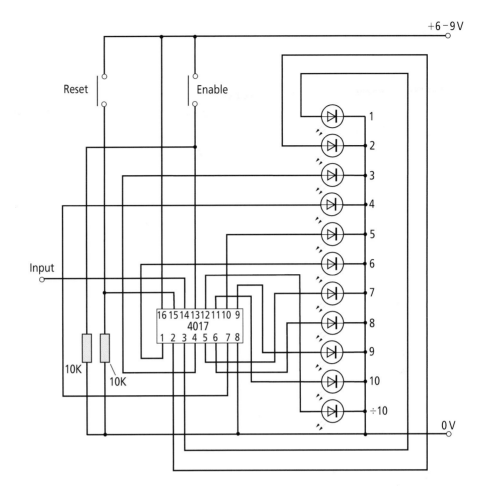

*A PCB mask and component layout for the circuit*

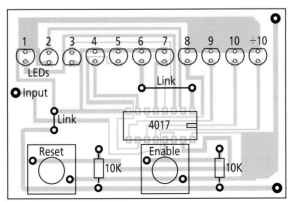

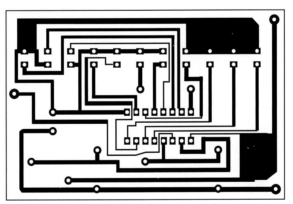

## ■ ACTIVITY

▶ Look at the circuit above and try to explain how it could be modified to reset automatically on each sixth input pulse.

▶ The IC can be used to make an electronic dice. Find out how to do this and draw a circuit diagram to show how the chip would be used.

## KEY POINTS

● Inputs to counters must be clean digital pulses.
● Schmitt triggers are used to produce clean signals and debounce switches.
● A 4017 IC can be used as a 10 event counter.

# Counting With Bistables

*Many electronic counters count the pulses they receive using a binary system, which uses only two digits, 1 and 0. The digits which make up a binary number are called bits, short for binary digits.*

## Binary Up-Counter

A simple binary counter which increases by one with each input can be made by linking a sequence of bistables together. Using four bistables in this way makes a four-bit indicator.

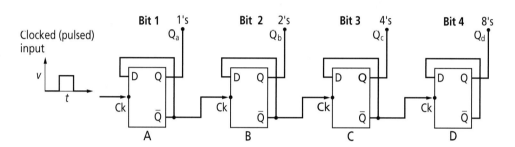

## How It Works

The counter uses D-type bistables (D stands for data). The input to the D connection controls the output states at the moment when the clock input is pulsed. If D is 'high', Q is 'high' and $\bar{Q}$ is 'low'. If D is 'low', Q is 'low' and $\bar{Q}$ is 'high'.

The Q output of each bistable is connected to the clock input of the next. The D (data) connection of each is connected to the $\bar{Q}$ output.

Connecting them in this way makes the outputs of the bistables change state on every pulse for bit A, every two pulses for bit B, every four pulses for C and every eight pulses for D.

## Counting in Binary

Binary counting uses a series of 0s and 1s to represent numbers. These 0s and 1s are read from right to left to give the decimal number equivalent.

Bit 1 can be 1 or 0. Bit 2 can be 2 or 0. Bit 3 can be 4 or 0. Bit 4 can be 8 or 0. A four-bit counter could count from 0000 to 1111 (decimal 15).

A count of 7 would show a 'high' output on A, B and C (read from right to left). D would remain 'low'. Binary 7 is written as 0111.

| Input pulse number | Output | | | |
|---|---|---|---|---|
| | Qd | Qc | Qb | Qa |
| 0 | 0 | 0 | 0 | 0 |
| 1 | 0 | 0 | 0 | 1 |
| 2 | 0 | 0 | 1 | 0 |
| 3 | 0 | 0 | 1 | 1 |
| 4 | 0 | 1 | 0 | 0 |
| 5 | 0 | 1 | 0 | 1 |
| 6 | 0 | 1 | 1 | 0 |
| 7 | 0 | 1 | 1 | 1 |
| 8 | 1 | 0 | 0 | 0 |
| 9 | | | | |
| 10 | | | | |
| 11 | | | | |
| 12 | | | | |
| 13 | | | | |
| 14 | | | | |
| 15 | | | | |

The truth table above shows how the outputs of each bit change with the input pulses.

Find out how to convert binary numbers to decimal numbers and vice versa.

**■ ACTIVITY**

Complete the table to show the states of the four outputs, Qa, Qb, Qc and Qd, for fifteen input pulses.

## 4013 IC

The 4013 IC has two independent D-type flip-flops (bistables) connected to the pins as shown. Each can store two bits of 0–15 binary. A practical version of the counter could be made with two of these ICs.

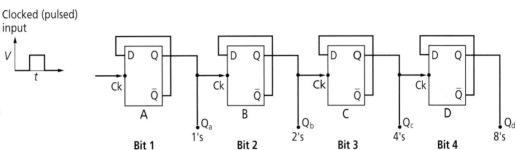

## Binary Down-Counter

A four-bit binary down-counter uses the $\bar{Q}$ output to connect to the clock input of the next bistable. In this case the count decreases by one for every input pulse.

A practical circuit diagram might look like the one at the bottom of the page.

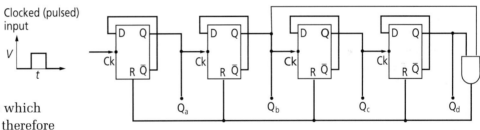

## BCD Counter

A BCD (binary-coded decimal) counter is a four-bit binary up-counter which counts 0–9 and then resets.

When the input count is 1010 (tenth pulse), Qd and Qb $= 1$. These act as inputs to the AND gate which resets all the bistables. The counter therefore resets to zero on the tenth count.

### KEY POINTS

- Binary up- or down-counters can be made by cascading (linking together) to D-type bistables.
- Four bistables connected together can count from 0 to 15 or 15 to 0.
- Numbers greater than 15 can be counted by connecting more bistables in series.
- Counters can be made to reset at desired numbers.
- BCD counters count 0–9 and then reset.

■ **ACTIVITY**

▶ Draw a practical circuit diagram for the counter. What would you use as output indicators?

▶ Note – pins 4, 6, 8 and 10 should be connected to 0V. The clock input must be clean and square waved, i.e. from a de-bounced circuit or astable.

■ **ACTIVITY**

▶ Make up the circuit on the left on prototype board. Think about how to arrange the LEDs to make the binary number easy to read.

▶ Redraw the BCD counter diagram to show how the counter could be made to reset on the sixth count.

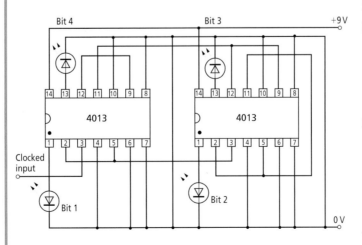

PCBs 'Я' US

*electronic components*

115

# Displaying Numbers

*One of the most common ways of displaying the output from a counter is to use a seven-segment display. Clock, digital radio and stereo equipment displays all use this type of indicator.*

## Seven-Segment Displays

Seven-segment LED displays consist of seven small LEDs arranged to produce the decimal numbers 0–9 when various combinations of the segments light up.

If the LED cathodes are joined together they are known as common cathode displays and the segments light with 'high' inputs – the common cathode connection is connected to 0 V.

### ■ ACTIVITY

Work out the decimal number that would be shown by the display if the inputs to the segments were as follows:

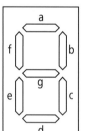

```
  a b c d e f g
1 1 1 1 1 1 1 0
2 1 0 1 1 0 1 1
3 1 1 1 0 0 0 0
```

The display is a common cathode type.

## A 0–9 Event Counter

One way of driving seven-segment displays is to use a 4026 IC. This chip is a decade counter with output suitable for directly driving low-current displays.

The circuit diagram shows how a 4026 IC could be used to drive a common cathode seven-segment display. In normal operation, pins 2 and 15 are connected to 0 V and pin 3 to +V. The input is connected to pin 1, and pins 6, 7, 9, 10, 11, 12 and 13 are connected to the display. Pin 5 is the 'carry'. The counter is reset to zero by taking pin 15 'high'.

The counter advances one count on each 'low' to 'high' pulse fed to the input. The input signal can be provided in many ways, e.g. an astable, a switch or a light sensor, but it must be a clean digital signal.

Taking pin 2 'high' stops the count.

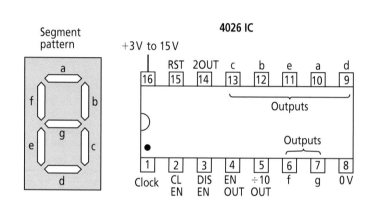

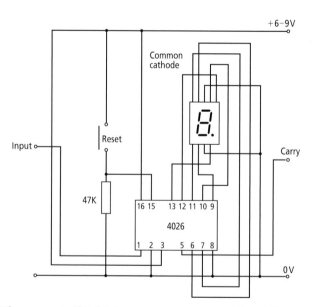

The carry is 'high' for counts 0 to 4 and 'low' for counts 5 to 9. It gives one output pulse for every ten input pulses and acts as a 'divide by ten' output. For counts greater than 9 this carry provides the input to a second counter/display system.

## Using a BCD Counter to Drive a Seven-Segment Display

BCD (binary-coded decimal) counters, such as the one shown on page 115, can also be used to drive seven-segment displays. The outputs A, B, C and D must be decoded via a BCD decoder chip which converts them into seven outputs (a, b, c, d, e, f, g) capable of driving the display.

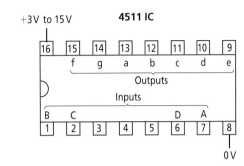

### 4511 IC

A 4511 IC is an example of a BCD decoder/display driver. The input pins are 1, 2, 6 and 7. The output to the seven-segment display is taken from pins 9–15.

The IC is usually used with pins 3 and 4 connected to +V and pin 5 to 0 V. The display should be of a common cathode type.

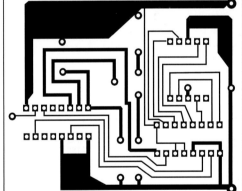

### Counter ICs

If you need to use a counter in your product development you might consider using an IC which has been designed to count in a specific way. The 4510 BCD IC is an up/down counter which can count up or down, and would be ideal for an electronic die.

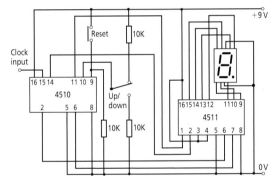

### 4510 IC

In normal use pins 5 and 9 are connected to 0 V.

Pin 15 is the input, and pins 2, 6, 11 and 14 are the outputs. If pin 10 is 'low' the counter counts up, and if it is 'high' it counts down.

Pin 7 is the 'carry' which allows the ICs to be cascaded for counts bigger than 9.

Pin 9 resets the counter if it is made 'high' momentarily.

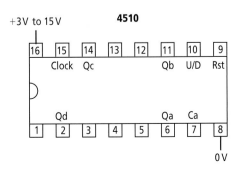

### KEY POINTS

Seven-segment displays:
- can be used to give decimal number outputs;
- are made up of small LEDs which light in different combinations;
- are operated by decoder/driver ICs.

### ■ ACTIVITY

Use a prototype board to check the operation of the circuit above. Experiment with pin 10.

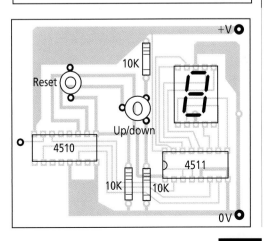

# Counting With a PIC

*A PIC (Peripheral Interface Controller) is very useful as it can replace many different components and increase the function of a circuit. This means circuits will use less components and their operation can be soon modified by changing the PIC's program.*

## Using a PIC in your project

There are many different PIC's available. A particularly useful one is the 16F84. This has eight output and five input pins. It must be correctly connected to work reliably.

The PIC requires a stabilised power supply of 6 volts and a 4MHz resonator to control the PIC's internal clock. A reset switch can be added which will allow the PIC program to be restarted.

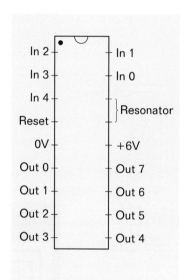

## Programming your PIC

There are a several commercially available systems suitable for use in school. It is best to draw a flow chart for your system before you start and map out how each of the pins will be used. You can then program the PIC and use a project board to check its operation before you build your own Printed Circuit Board (PCB). Two program styles can be used, either a flow chart that uses symbols or a list of instructions to be followed by the PIC. Each line must have its own identity code. Some systems need a computer, while others are standalone.

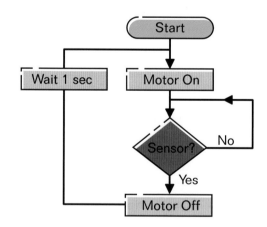

### ■ ACTIVITIES

► Write a program to control a series of eight LED's so they form an interesting visual display.
► Write a program that could be used with a PIC that would control a pedestrian crossing.
► Use a component catalogue to identify other PIC's that have a different range of INPUTS and OUTPUTS.

## Input Switch

A digital input signal can be sent to a PIC by using a switch, such as a micro-switch or reed switch. These can be used as sensors in a more complex program. The switches need to be connected to the PIC as shown below.

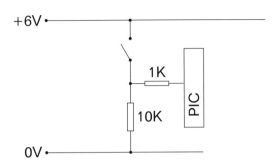

## The Seven-segment Display

The output current from a PIC is quite small but will switch on an LED. The Seven-segment display uses seven small LED's. When these are switched on in the correct sequence they form the decimal numbers 0 to 9, as well as letters. It is possible to use seven of the OUTPUT pins to control the display. You could use a Macro or Sub-routine to switch the correct LEDs on for each number or letter.

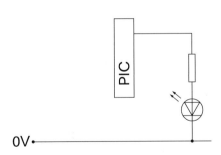

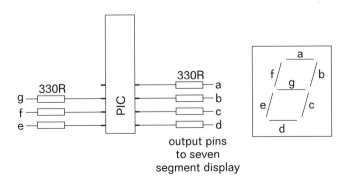

output pins
to seven
segment display

## Component Redundancy

A circuit using a PIC and six LEDs could be used as a dice and will use less components. However just by changing the program it could also be used as a timer or metronome. This increases the flexibility of the circuit and helps manufacturers produce a range of different products. Just by changing the program and using a different case a new product could soon be produced.

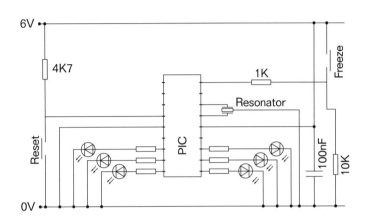

### ■ ACTIVITIES

1 Programme a PIC to count input pulse from a micro-switch. When it reaches ten, all the LEDs should flash on and off three times.
2 Write a program for a PIC so it will operate as an electronic egg timer. The timer period could be controlled by a series of different input switches. The PIC would then count done every minute by using a series of LEDs. Rewrite the program so it will operate as a metronome.

### IN YOUR PROJECT

Draw the final circuit diagram for a PIC and program it so it can be used as an electronic dice. Explain the advantages of using a PIC when compared to a series of electronic components.

### KEY POINTS

● A PIC can be used to replace several components; this is called component redundancy.
● Using a different program can soon change a PICs operation; this increases the functionality of the circuit.
● A Seven-segment displays uses small LEDs to display a digital number from a PIC.

# Cutting and Shaping Plastics

*The two plastics you are most likely to use for making your product models are acrylic and polystyrene. Both have various advantages and disadvantages. Working with either demands precision and accuracy to achieve successful results.*

You could use a CNC engraving machine to cut out more complex shapes.

| Material | Advantages | Disadvantages |
|---|---|---|
| Acrylic | – quality feel<br>– wide range of colours, including transparent<br>– can be bent accurately<br>– can be polished, including cut edges | – fairly brittle<br>– does not vacuum form easily (if you need to vacuum form acrylic, e.g. for transparent shapes, then use cast acrylic) |
| Polystyrene | – vacuum forms very well, giving an industrial process advantage (can be repeated)<br>– can be fabricated quickly and easily | – difficult to bend (tends to stretch when heated)<br>– does not polish very well<br>– does not machine sand easily (tends to melt) |

## Cutting Acrylic Sheet

You can cut sheet plastic using a hacksaw, a coping saw or a scroll saw. A scoll saw achieves complex shapes quickly and easily.

You may find the plastic 'welds' itself back together behind the blade. Covering the top surface with masking tape will help overcome this and also gives a protective surface that lends itself well to accurate marking out.

*Score to a depth of about 0.5mm using a number of light strokes (this avoids 'skidding' off the straight edge).*

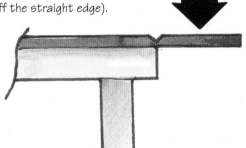

Straight-line cuts can be achieved by scoring and snapping. Use a specially designed blade or ask your teacher if one could be made out of an old mechanical hacksaw blade.

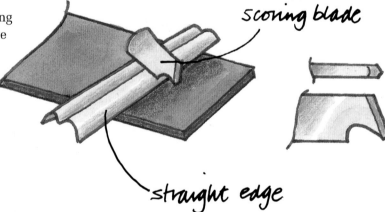

*scoring blade*

*straight edge*

*Hold the sheet firmly with the score line upwards and on the edge of the bench (or short pieces can be held in the vice) and carefully press down and the plastic will snap. Practise this first on some scrap pieces.*

## Polystyrene

Polystyrene can be cut and assembled quickly and easily, but requires precision and accuracy if you are to make successful product models.

### ■ ACTIVITY

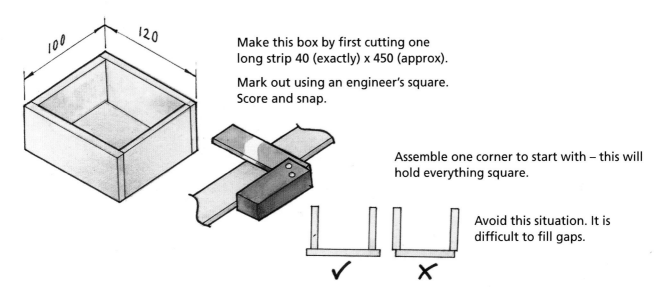

Make this box by first cutting one long strip 40 (exactly) x 450 (approx).

Mark out using an engineer's square. Score and snap.

Assemble one corner to start with – this will hold everything square.

Avoid this situation. It is difficult to fill gaps.

The pieces need to be bonded together using a suitable solvent.
▶ Apply the solvent to both surfaces first.
▶ Assemble one side to the base and run in some solvent.
▶ Add each side one at a time, using the sides to hold each other square.
▶ The solvent will hold the pieces quickly but full bonding takes time.

## Line-Bending Acrylic

A line bender localises the heat using a strip heating element. This 'crispens up' the folded edge.

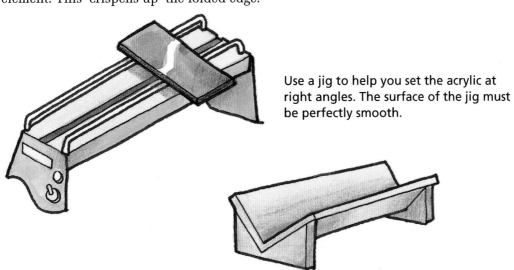

Use a jig to help you set the acrylic at right angles. The surface of the jig must be perfectly smooth.

**IN YOUR PROJECT**

▶ 2–3 mm polystyrene is best for fabricating.
▶ Polystyrene solvent is best for bonding your product case, but avoid the fumes by using in a well-ventilated area.
▶ Cut to the exact size to avoid having to sand after cutting.
▶ Remember – the solvent melts the surface as well!
▶ Polystyrene melts rather than sands on a belt or disc sander.
▶ Remember to check for squareness both when cutting and assembling.

# Vacuum Forming

*Most electronic products have plastic casings. These can be made by vacuum forming high density polystyrene sheet.*

Vacuum forming offers the following advantages:

▷ a rigid shape that requires no fabrication;
▷ a repeatable shape (you can take a number off the same mould);
▷ a variety of details can be built into the mould;
▷ complicated rounded shapes can be achieved by adding details such as large radii to the corners.

## Detail Design

Shallow surface detail can be added to a mould using thick cardboard or thin MDF. It can be functional or purely decorative.

This involved three layers of card, one complete surface with a circle missing and a second strip of card.

These details were achieved from three cuts made in one piece of card which was then separated.

Don't forget to allow for the draft angle if the dimensions are critical.

A separate moulding could be designed to fit inside your product to hold the various components.

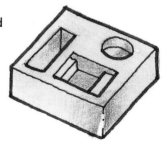

To find out more about plastic, go to:
**www.materials-database.co.uk**

## Plastic Manufacturing Methods

The advantages that plastic products have over many wood and metal products is that they can be fabricated as complete components which require little or no finishing.

There are two main types of plastic:

▷ thermosets such as polystyrene, polythene and acrylic which soften when heated and can be recycled;

▷ thermoplastics such as epoxies, polyester resin and melamine that can only be moulded once.

**IN YOUR PROJECT**

When specifying a suitable plastic manufacturing process for your product you will need to consider:
▶ the design of the component;
▶ the design of the tool or mould;
▶ the processing characteristics of the plastic;
▶ the advantages and limitation of each process.

**IN YOUR PROJECT**

▶ Avoid making your mould too deep as the plastic will thin badly making the case very weak.
▶ The greater the draft angle the easier the plastic moulding will come off the mould.
▶ Build in as many features as you can, such as fixings for components or lids etc.
▶ If you can avoid damaging the surface of the moulding you can take advantage of the plastic sheet's high quality surface.
▶ It is important to finish the mould to a high standard. Any blemishes will appear on the surface of the moulded plastic and could make it difficult to separate the mould and the plastic.
▶ The mould should be left in its natural state. Any surface finishes, e.g. wax or cellulose sealer, may react when in contact with the hot plastic.

| Process | Advantages | Limitations | Typical products |
|---|---|---|---|
| THERMOPLASTICS Injection moulding | High-volume production (200 000+). Low unit cost. Excellent surface finish. Little waste. Large range of sizes possible, up to cars and boat shells. | Initial high investment in machine tools. Closed container shapes can only be produced by additional assembly. Complex shapes are difficult and expensive. | Most high-precision plastic components. Plastic clips, cases, knobs, buttons, handles, toothbrushes. |
| Vacuum forming | Relatively cheap machine tools. | Stretching of plastic sheet can thin corners. | Egg containers, margarine tubs, disposable cups, larger shapes such as a board game. |
| Blow moulding | High volume, high production rate. Good quality complete products. | Surface finish not as good as injection moulding. Requires thin film, so not suitable for high-density castings. | Bottles and containers, e.g. for detergent, shampoo, soft drinks. |
| Extrusion | Relatively fast, suitable for high-volume production. Wide range of possible sections. Precision and surface finish good. | Range of diameter section 25–200 mm. Machines are initially expensive. | Tubes, rods, sheets of continuous length, producing materials for blow moulding. |
| THERMOSETS Compression moulding | Good surface finish, high-volume production. Most suitable for high-density, heat-resistant components. | Expensive machine tools. Excess material (the flash) has to be trimmed off adding to material and labour cost. | Temperature-resistant products such as kettles. Hardwearing sheet materials. |

■ **ACTIVITY**

Fnd out more about how these processes work. Write brief notes on each process and draw simple diagrams of the types of machine tools required.

**PCBs 'Я' US**

*resistant materials*

# Manufacturing With Other Materials

*Most electronic products are made of injection-moulded thermoplastics. It is, however, also possible to use a wide variety of other materials for manufacturing.*

## Wood and Manufactured Board

Solid timber gives a quality feel to products. However, it is quite expensive and labour intensive to process. You could use it for decorative features on your product.

Manufactured boards include plywood, chipboard and MDF (medium density fibre) board. These are used for some electronic products, such as speaker cabinets and other items of audio equipment.

▷ **Plywood**: birch-faced ply is a high quality plywood, light in colour and ideal for making toys. It takes coloured stains and varnishes well.

▷ **Chipboard** has the advantage of being cheap and stable, i.e. it does not warp or twist. It is not a very attractive material, however, and normally has a veneer finish or a plastic 'foil' applied to the surface (woodgrain or plain).

▷ **MDF**: very close textured MDF is useful for making moulds for vacuum forming. It can be used for fabricating boxes, and should be assembled using PVA wood glue. Avoid using panel pins which will split the board. You will need to work accurately. MDF can be painted, but requires a number of coats to give an acceptable finish. Try using about three coats of cellulose sanding sealer before applying a spray paint finish.

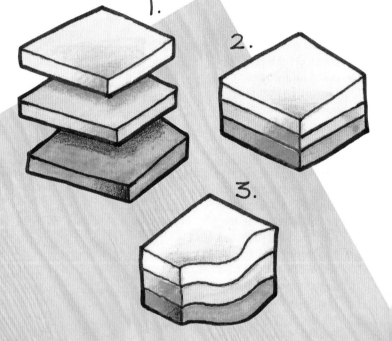

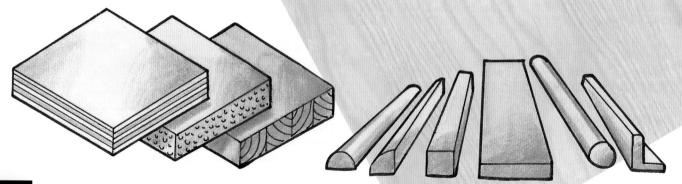

## Finishing

The sort of impression your product will make depends on this final process. Remember to allocate plenty of time for preparing the metal, using emery cloth for steel and silicon carbide paper on aluminium. A coat of paint will only be as good as the surface underneath it: trouble taken at this point will pay off!

▷ Mild steel is strong and versatile but requires finishing to avoid rusting. To paint steel, remove all surface blemishes including rust, and degrease before spray painting, including a primer. It can be hand painted using a one-coat paint.

▷ Oil blacking is an alternative finish for steel. This involves heating the steel to a dull red and then quenching in oil. It gives a blue/black 'high-tech' look but is not a very hardwearing finish and is only moderately resistant to corrosion.

▷ Aluminium can be polished to a dull shine, or a 'brushed' finish can be achieved using a medium grade silicon carbide paper on the surface. It is important to work it in one direction only.

Spraying the finished article with silicon polish will help prevent it tarnishing.

 **ICT** ➜ You could use a CD-Rom encyclopaedia to find out more about materials.

## Metals

Metals are valuable materials for making electronic products. They are particularly useful where strength is important, especially for brackets and fixings.

▷ **Mild steel** comes in a variety of forms. Sheet steel can be used for making strong cases and a variety of brackets and fixings. Bright drawn mild steel comes as round, square and flat bar as well as tubes and angle.

Mild steel can be cut and machined to produce components such as pivots. One of its major advantages is the range of permanent joining methods it accepts – welding, brazing and silver solder.

▷ **Aluminium** is a light and, in its natural state, fairly soft metal. It comes in the same forms as steel and can be cast. Find out if your school has the facility to do this. If weight is an important factor in your product specification, then aluminium may be the solution. However, it is a lot softer and more expensive than steel.

The main disadvantage of aluminium is that it cannot be welded without specialist equipment. It therefore has to be joined mechanically using nuts and bolts, rivets, etc.

Alternatively it can be bonded very successfully using epoxy resin (follow the manufacturer's instructions).

*Clean off blemishes with files*

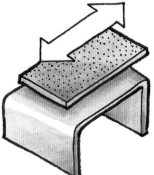

*Emery cloth used in one direction only*

# Going Into Production

*The quicker and easier it is to make something, the more can be made, and the cheaper it becomes to make them. As you develop your design ideas you will need to think carefully about how the various parts of your product would be manufactured most effectively.*

*What type of production would be most suitable for your design project?*

### One-off

It might take an hour for someone to solder a set of components onto a single PCB. This is called single unit or 'one-off' production.

### Batch

If three people work together, sharing the tasks and the manufacturing equipment, they could make twenty identical boards in four hours. They might then switch quickly to making a different design of board to meet market demand. This is known as batch production.

### Mass

If a number of workers organise themselves and their workplace appropriately, then they might easily be able to make ten or more boards an hour, eight hours a day, for weeks on end. This process is called mass production.

### Continuous

Continuous production is when the production process is set up to make one specific product 24 hours a day, 7 days a week, possibly over periods of many years, such as in some food processing and chemical manufacturing industries.

## Mixed Methods

Most production processes involve a mixture of these methods. Some parts might need to be individually or batch produced, while others will be run off continuously.

Different types of manufacturing equipment are needed for the different processes. Some require special-purpose tools, made to suit a particular product. Others require basic machines with parts which, to a greater or lesser extent, can be changed and reprogrammed when necessary to make different shapes and forms.

# 'Buying In' Components

*An important part of the electronic product manufacturing process involves calculating and obtaining the correct quantity of components needed from outside suppliers.*

You could use a spreadsheet to calculate the cost of your product, and how the cost would vary depending on the number required.

## Electronic Components

### Preferred values

Resistors are made in a range of values known as the preferred value series. This lists the different resistances available. One example is the E12 series which is 10, 12, 15, 18, 22, 27, 33, 39, 47, 56, 68 and 82, and these values times 10, 100, 1000, 10 000, 100 000, 1000 000.

### Relays

Relays come in a wide variety of forms. When specifying relays useful data includes: type, size, contact type, maximum contact current, coil-operating voltage.

### Transistors (bipolar)

The main information you need when specifying transistors is the type, the type of case (this tells you which leg is which), the gain and the maximum collector/emitter current.

See page 46 for more information about transistors.

Most suppliers produce catalogues which provide performance data about the electronic components they sell.

| Type | Price | | | Poly/Mat | Case | Vcb (max.) V | Vce (max.) V | Veb (max.) V | Ic (max.) mA | Ptot (max.) mW | hFE (min.) @ Ic (mA) |
|------|-------|------|------|----------|------|------|------|------|------|------|------|
| | 1+ | 100+ | 500+ | | | | | | | | |
| AC127 | 0.45 | 0.38 | 0.30 | NG | T01 | 32 | 12 | 10 | 500 | 340 | 50@500 |
| AC128 | 0.45 | 0.38 | 0.30 | PG | T01 | 32 | 16 | 10 | 1A | 267 | 45@1A |
| AD161 | 0.80 | 0.68 | 0.62 | NG | X03 | 32 | 20 | 10 | 1A | 4W | 80@500 |
| BC107 | 0.10 | 0.085 | 0.08 | NS | T018 | 50 | 45 | 6 | 100 | 300 | 125@2 |
| BC107B | 0.12 | 0.10 | 0.09 | NS | T018 | 50 | 45 | 6 | 100 | 300 | 330@2 |
| BC108 | 0.10 | 0.065 | 0.08 | NS | T018 | 30 | 20 | 5 | 100 | 300 | 125@2 |
| BC108B | 0.11 | 0.105 | 0.085 | NS | T018 | 30 | 20 | 5 | 100 | 300 | 330@2 |
| BC108C | 0.12 | 0.105 | 0.095 | NS | T018 | 30 | 20 | 5 | 100 | 300 | 500@2 |
| BC109 | 0.11 | 0.09 | 0.085 | NS | T018 | 30 | 20 | 5 | 100 | 300 | 180@2 |
| BC109C | 0.12 | 0.105 | 0.095 | NS | T039 | 30 | 20 | 5 | 100 | 300 | 420@2 |

TO18 CASE

Collector  Base  Emitter

## Fittings and Fastenings

There are a variety of screw, rivet and other fastenings you can use with your product.

▶ Coarse-threaded screws, such as self-tapping screws and screws designed for use with manufactured board, also work well with high density polystyrene. Drill a pilot hole the same diameter as the core of the screw, which will cut its own thread.
▶ Choose screws that are BZP (bright zinc plated). You can also find fastenings with a black finish, which blends well with some products.
▶ Pop rivets work well with aluminium.
▶ Press covers are designed to fit into Pozidriv screws. Not only do they neaten up a product but if used on the underside they make ideal feet.
▶ Connecta bolts are designed for assembling chipboard furniture. They could be adapted for assembling an electronic product.

▶ Cable duct, designed to be used with speaker cable, has a self-adhesive fixing which could easily be adapted for other uses.

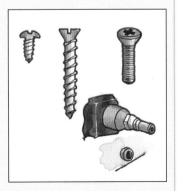

## ■ ACTIVITY

Go to a DIY superstore if you can and look at the vast range of DIY fixtures and fittings that are available. You will discover some good ideas for hardware you could use or adapt for your project.

### KEY POINTS

● You should use data to help you choose components.
● Resistor values are identified by colour coding.
● Resistors are made in preferred value series.

# Computer-Aided Design

*Computer-aided design (CAD) systems make it quicker and easier to create an image of an intended product than modelling using conventional 3D construction methods. This means that new ideas can be tried out, modified and evaluated more quickly.*

## Methods of Representation

There are three main ways of representing a 3D object on a computer.

▷ Wire frame modelling means that the object is represented by a series of lines. 'Hidden' lines can be removed to enhance the image.

▷ Surface modelling is a feature which adds colour, shading and texture to produce a surface to the wire frame model. This gives a stronger sense of the 3D form.

▷ Solid modelling works by basing the image on geometric shapes such as circles, cones and rectangles which are then 'morphed' together to produce the final shape. The computer image can be explored for information on mass, volume, centre of gravity and stress analysis.

**ICT** →

### AKA Mobile Phone

The first stage was to create two appearance proposals for the design of this new portable telephone. These were presented as hand-made models. The models were made from a material called Ureol which is a resin that can be cut and finished easily by hand.

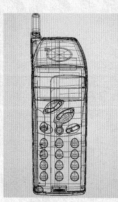

Next AKA were commissioned to combine the designs and the technical specification into a viable product. Alias software was used to create digital models of all the electronic components and to then wrap a 3D 'skin' round them. Buttons were positioned to ensure existing components could be used, saving development time and costs. Shaded images of the wireframe were constantly assessed to ensure that the model met the aesthetic as well as technical requirements.

AKA then created a physical model to present to the client. This one was made directly from the computer data using a CNC milling machine.

A Rapid Prototype was produced to check that all the electronic components and plastic housing fitted correctly. This was created using a laser cutting a liquid resin, again fully computer controlled from the original computer data. Fully rendered colour images were then created. Colours, textures and graphics were assigned to the surfaces of the digital model and photorealistic images created. These pictures were used in brochures and advertising posters for the product launch. Finally the 3D digital data was sent via modem directly to a toolmaker in Seoul, Korea where the production tools were made.

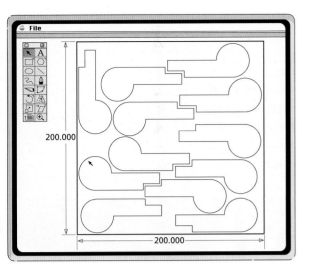

**IN YOUR PROJECT**

Can CAD help you try out alternative shapes and layouts for your electronic products? Find out more about the different types of CAD available.

## Nesting

The economic use of materials is vital for commercial success. CAD can help with laying out the cutting template to ensure minimum wastage. Rotating sections into different layouts is simple.

## Component Layout

2D programs can also be useful in testing the layout of components in a design. The computer stores the relationships between components, such as tolerances, and takes them into account when objects are moved around.

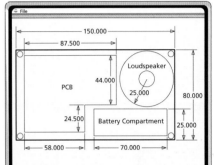

## Electronic Circuit Design

Electronic 'workshops' enable the user to model electronic circuits and to explore their behaviour without needing to build them from real components. This can avoid expensive errors at the design stage.

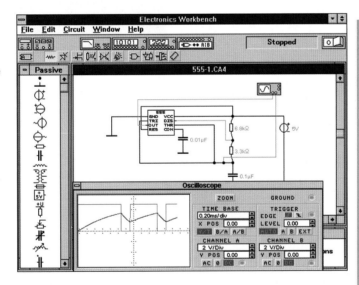

**KEY POINTS**

Using CAD has a number of advantages:
● speeding up the process of design development and, as a result, the number of designs which can be produced;
● providing accurate information on how a design will function under different conditions, prior to expensive 3D prototyping;
● enabling changes to be made quickly which can then be communicated throughout the team working on the production;
● storing design information easily and retrieving it on a database;
● transmitting information anywhere in the world in seconds.

## PCB Design

A library of tracks and component configurations allows the copper track and pad pattern to be laid out on the screen. The resulting mask can then be printed out and processed using photo-resist methods or the design transferred to a CAD/CAM machine for direct manufacture (see page 132). A milling machine is used to cut away the unwanted copper from the board.

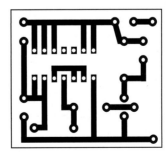

ICT

Remember that it is illegal to make copies of computer programs, unless you have the appropriate licence from the software manufacturer.

# Making It By Computer

*More and more production processes can now be done by machines which are controlled by computers. Automated manufacturing is safer, quicker, more reliable and eventually cheaper than conventional production methods.*

## Computer-Aided Manufacture (CAM)

CAM is a term used to describe the process whereby parts of products are manufactured by equipment which is controlled by a computer. One of the restrictions of batch production is that after relatively few products have been made, a machine has to be reset to the requirements of a different product. The main advantage of CAM is that the new instructions are stored electronically and can be downloaded and programmed into the machine very quickly. This also means it is easier to make small changes to the design to suit changes in the market, or to produce specialised short-run products for individual clients.

Where computer-aided manufacture is used to replace a manual operation, greater productivity is possible, because the machine can work continuously. Also, the quality is more consistent and fewer faulty goods are produced. CAM systems can also work with materials and chemicals which might be harmful to human operators.

*Industrial robots (which look nothing like a person!) can be programmed to perform a variety of tasks using a range of tools and materials*

*Automated and autonomous guided vehicles can be used to transport components, tools and materials to the appropriate assembly area*

## Computer Numerically Controlled (CNC) Manufacture

▷ CNC milling machines can cut shapes from plastics, metal and wood.
▷ CNC engraving machines are often used to cut the track pattern from copper-clad boards.
▷ CNC drilling machines can drill preset patterns rapidly and very accurately.
▷ CNC assembly machines can place electronic components onto a printed circuit board. These are used where the demand is in excess of 2000 components an hour and use surface-mounted components (SMD) rather than the leaded devices you use in your products.
▷ CNC test units can check the function of assembled PCBs.

Machine tools can be programmed independently, but also have the facility to exchange data with other computers. They can therefore become part of a complex automated production system.

*Once assembled all the soldering is done at the same time using a carefully controlled heating system*

## Computer Integrated Manufacture (CIM)

Computer technology has enabled the development of CIM. World class manufacturing techniques use computers extensively to control or organise all aspects of manufacture from design to distribution. Manufacturing companies which have adopted such systems have been able to reduce dramatically the time it takes them to design and make their products, and to increase their quality and reliability. This gives them a significant advantage over their competitors.

ICT ⟶

You could use a CNC machine to make part of your case.

**IN YOUR PROJECT**

Geometric shapes and graphics produced on a computer screen can be downloaded onto a CNC vinyl film cutter which cuts the shape from coloured plastic film. Applied to your product the cut film can add colour and styling detail.

**KEY POINTS**

● CNC milling machines can cut flat plastic shapes for manufacture of 3D forms. Straight lines and curves are cut with great accuracy. They are also useful for the manufacture of internal components and for adding surface detail.
● CNC lathes can turn, drill and cut components for small batch production from metal and plastic.
● CNC engravers can cut PCB layouts.

PCBs 'R' US

*manufacturing*

# Manufacturing PCBs

*Once you have developed an electronic solution you may decide to produce it as a circuit mounted on a PCB. Simple circuits can be drawn and etched from copper-coated sheets. Photo-resist boards are commonly used to produce high quality PCBs for more complex circuits.*

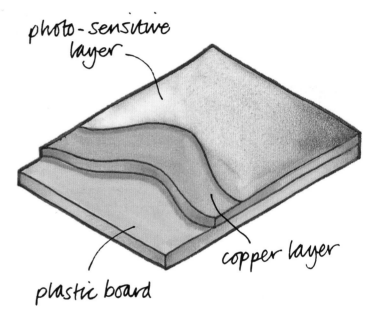

*PCB CAD packages enable you to design circuits and to simplify them automatically on screen, and then to print the PCB mask out directly*

## Direct Etching

A single PCB can be produced by direct etching of copper-clad board. The mask is 'drawn' directly on top of the board using etch-resist pens or rub-down transfers. Simple boards can be made cheaply using strips of sticky-back plastic for the mask.

## Photographic Transfer

PCBs are also made from photo-resist board – a rigid plastic sheet bonded to a layer of copper which is, in turn, covered with a light-sensitive chemical layer. The board is usually covered with a peel-off layer of black plastic. Why do you think this is important?

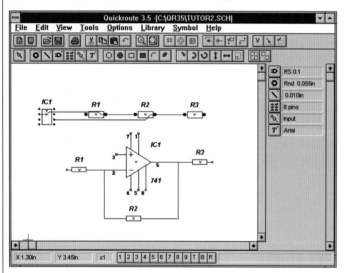

### ICT ➡

You could use CAM to produce your PCB, either by using a vinly cutter to make a mask or by machining the copper clad board.

*photo-sensitive layer*

*copper layer*

*plastic board*

The pattern of tracks and pads is transferred to the board by creating a photographic image on the photo-sensitive layer. The image is produced from a PCB mask.

## Designing the Mask

The pcb mask consists of a series of lines (tracks) and connecting points (pads) which will form the copper connections between the circuit components. A typical PCB mask is shown here.

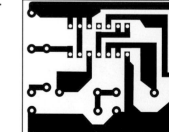

When designing the mask you need to imagine the circuit connections without the components in place. Remember – the components don't usually look like their symbol.

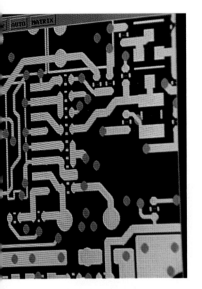

Good design should result in a compact board with few wire links. Make sure that tracks are not too close together, do not cross if they are supposed to be separate, and that spaces left for components are big enough for them to fit easily.

Don't make pads too small and tracks too narrow as they tend to shrink during processing.

## From Photo-Resist Board to PCB

This manufacturing process involves five main activities – producing the mask, exposing the board, developing the board, etching the board and cleaning and drilling the board.

### KEY POINTS

- PCBs can be produced using photo-resist board.
- This process uses a mask to create the copper track and pad pattern.
- The mask can be used more than once to produce multiple copies of the board.
- There are ICT packages available to help you design masks.
- ICT generated masks can be modified easily if required.

## 1 Produce mask

If the mask has been generated using a PCB Designer, print out onto a transparent sheet using a laser printer. If this is not possible, photocopy the printout from a dot matrix or bubble jet printer onto an acetate sheet.

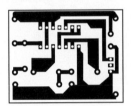

## 2 Expose board

Place mask on UV box glass, face up, and cover with suitable piece of photo-resist board (sensitive layer in contact with mask), close lid and switch on UV. For acetate masks the exposure time varies from around $2\frac{1}{2}$ to 7 minutes.

## 3 Develop exposed board

Develop board in developer solution. Take care! Make sure you use tongs as the solution is strongly alkaline. Leave the board until the exposed photo-resist layer is washed off leaving copper surface. Timing is important – too little time will not fully remove the exposed layer; too much time and the non-exposed surface will also wash off. Remember to rinse the board.

## 4 Etch board

The developed board is etched by placing in ferric chloride solution until all of the exposed copper is dissolved. Use bubble etch tank to speed up the process. Take care! The solution is an irritant – use tongs and wear gloves and goggles when inserting and removing boards. Remember to rinse the board.

## 5 Clean and drill

Smooth edges of board with sandpaper and drill holes for components.

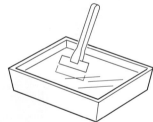

## PCB Mask Planner

You may find a mask planning sheet useful. Ask if your school has one which you can photocopy.

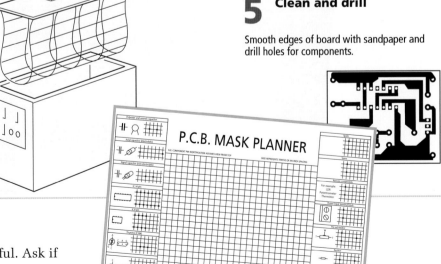

P.C.B. MASK PLANNER

# Quality Counts (1)

*Manufacturers need to ensure that all the products they are making are of acceptable quality. A range of tools and techniques have been developed to help check and maintain quality over a long production run.*

## Checking Components

Circuits sometimes do not work because of faulty components. A multimeter, set on the ohms range, can be used to check many common components such as bulbs, transistors, resistors, LEDs, diodes and relays.

When set on the d.c. volts range, a multimeter can also be used to check whether the voltages at certain points in a circuit are what they should be. For instance, if the base connection of an npn transistor is at around 1 V or more, the collector should be close to 0 V.

Multimeters can be used to check the voltage across components, and to check their resistance.

How does a digital multimeter differ from an analogue one?

*A technician tests components on electronic circuit boards*

*Close inspection of a circuit board. The technician wears magnifying goggles and protective gloves*

**Testing a 6V bulb**

Meter reads about 50 ohms
(polarity unimportant)

**Testing an LED**

Meter reads about 30 ohms
(note polarity)

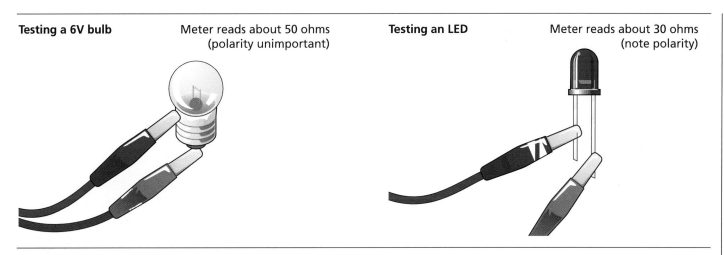

**Testing a diode**

Forward biased – meter
reads about 8 ohms

Reverse biased – meter
reads infinite resistance

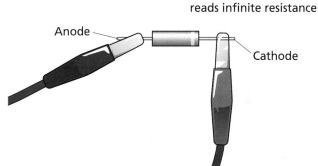

Anode

Cathode

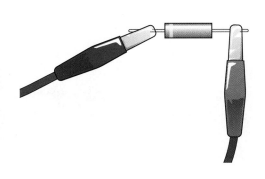

Any deviation from the above
readings proves the diode is unserviceable

**Testing an npn
transistor (BC108)**

Base – collector reading
meter reads about 10 ohms

Base – emitter reading
meter reads about 10 ohms

Collector          Emitter

Base

Collector          Emitter

Base

All other readings should show infinite on the meter. (i.e. Black lead to collector – red lead to base; black lead to emitter –
red lead to base; black lead to collector – red lead to emitter; black lead to emitter – red lead to collector.)

■ **ACTIVITY**

Use a multimeter to test
the range of components
shown above.

**KEY POINTS**

● The most common
reasons for circuits
not working are
poor soldering,
incorrect components,
poor design and
component and pcb
failure.

● A multimeter can be
used to test for faults.

# Quality Counts (2)

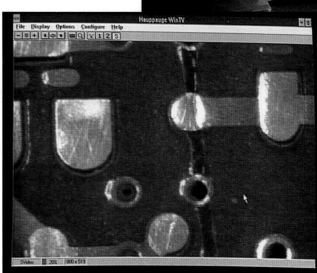

## Working to Tolerance

Have you ever tried making something exactly to size? What you produced would almost certainly have been out by fractions of a millimetre. How accurate does the manufacturing need to be so that the components will fit together?

The answer to this question is known as the tolerance limit – the acceptable deviation from the ideal size. It is expressed by two numbers: an upper and lower limit.

In a simple example it might be stated that a component intended to be 100 mm in length could vary between 99.1 mm and 100.9 mm. The tolerance is the difference between the upper and lower tolerance limits, i.e. 0.18 mm, or $+/-0.9$ mm. The specification for a product should include a statement about its tolerance limits.

Tolerances are important to ensure reliability, which in turn means fewer products are wasted during manufacture. The smaller the tolerance the better, but achieving greater accuracy requires careful measurement and skill in controlling tools, both of which can increase the cost considerably.

*Testing procedures are needed to ensure items are within the stated tolerance limits. New automated and computer-based equipment tends to be quicker and more efficient at producing and testing components which are finely toleranced*

## Quality Control

Manufacturers need to ensure that all the products they are making are of acceptable quality. At the most basic level, all products can be checked to ensure they are satisfactory.

A more sophisticated approach is to implement a system of quality control. This involves inspecting components as they are made, and gathering and analysing records.

In simple terms, a sample of components (say 1 in every 100) is subjected to rigorous tests which identify and record how far each item deviates from its target. Provided a component is found to be within acceptable limits, production continues. By examining the pattern of a series of tests, it may be noticed that a particular machine is producing increasing numbers of components which are close to the acceptable tolerance limits. It is then possible to adjust or, if necessary, repair the machine before it starts to produce items which would have to be classed as defective, possibly resulting in the production line being shut down.

The aim of quality control is therefore to achieve zero defects by being able to predict the failure of a machine.

The use of automated testing machines and of electronic gathering and analysis of data leads to higher standards of quality and less waste.

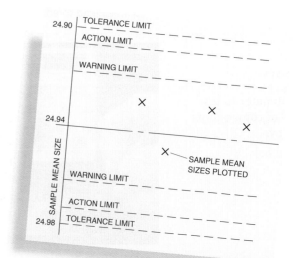

# Quality Assurance

What is good quality? This can be a difficult question to answer. A good quality product is not necessarily expensive, or one which lasts for ever. At one level we might say that a product that does what it is supposed to do and is safe is of good quality.

From a consumer's point of view a product is of good quality if it is felt to be good value for money. From a manufacturer's perspective, quality is about making good, value-for-money products in the most efficient way, and therefore at the most economical price.

Quality assurance is the overall approach taken by a company to ensure high standards of quality. It includes developing and monitoring standards, procedures, documentation and communication across the company as a whole. Usually a quality manual is produced which contains all the relevant information to guide staff.

Quality does not just happen – it has to be planned for and managed. Total quality management (or TQM) is an approach to management which aims to maximise the human

and physical resources of an organisation in the most cost-effective way to meet the needs and

expectations of the customer and the community.

## IN YOUR PROJECT

▶ How accurately do the different parts of your design need to be made?
▶ Which components need to fit together most accurately?

## KEY POINTS

● The design specification for a component should include statements about its tolerance limits.
● Tolerances are important to ensure reliability, which in turn reduces wastage of products during manufacture.
● The smaller the tolerance, the higher the manufacturing cost.

# British Standards

The British Standards Institute was the first national standards body in the world. Its main purpose is to draw up voluntary standards to be observed, and it produces documents which clarify the essential technical requirements for a product, material or process to be fit for its purpose.

There are a range of over 10 000 British Standards for almost every industry from food to building construction, and textiles to toys, and they cover all aspects of production, from materials to management.

Certification that a product manufacturing or management process conforms to a stated British Standard provides assurance that an acceptable quality can be expected, greatly reducing the risk of buying goods and services which could be defective in some way.

To find out more about safety standards, go to:
**www.bsi-global.com**

## IN YOUR PROJECT

▶ At what stage of manufacture would you recommend that a sample of your product should be tested for accuracy?
▶ What inspection and measurement tests could be carried out?
▶ How often should they be done?

## KEY POINTS

● Quality control systems help manufacturers reduce wastage and delay in production.
● They do this by predicting failure before it happens.
● Quality control forms a specific part of a programme of quality assurance.

# Controlling Hazards and Risk

*The world is a dangerous place. As designers and manufacturers produce new products, they need to ensure that they will be safe to use, and also safe to make.*

CORROSIVE

## ■ ACTIVITIES

▶ List aspects of the Health and Safety at Work Act which are relevant to the workshop you work in.
▶ What substances would need to be considered under COSHH regulations? Obtain hazard information from suppliers' catalogues or from a safety database.

Whilst designers must ensure that products conform to all the relevant safety standards they also need to be aware of the health and safety issues associated with manufacture.

There are four main areas to consider to help avoid potential accidents:

▷ the design of machinery and tools being used in the manufacturing process;
▷ the physical layout of the work area;
▷ the training of the workforce;
▷ the safety devices and procedures.

## Hazards and Risks

In the manufacturing process there are a series of regulations and codes of practice which must be observed, such as COSHH – the Control of Substances Hazardous to Health Regulations as well as the Health and Safety at Work Act.

Key considerations include:

▷ harmful fumes or particles;
▷ a high standard of hygiene and cleanliness;
▷ adequate heating, lighting and ventilation and minimum noise levels.

It is also essential to reduce the number of potential hazards – unsafe practices or conditions – which could occur in the workplace. Accidents are extremely costly in terms of personal distress, compensation and lost production.

## Risk Assessment

Although we cannot avoid risk, we can take steps to assess the likelihood of something happening, and minimise its impact if it does. Risk is not the same as uncertainty, which occurs where there is not enough information to evaluate the amount of risk involved.

When a production process involves hazardous situations it is necessary to analyse and assess each particular risk situation and ensure that adequate precautions are taken to minimise the potential danger. A substance which is hazardous can be used in such a way that the actual risk to anyone using it is reduced to a minimum.

**IN YOUR PROJECT**

▶ Identify those aspects of the production of your design that might be hazardous while your product is being manufactured or while you are making your product in school.
▶ What steps would you recommend be taken to minimise the risks, and why?

PCBs 'Я' US

*health and safety*

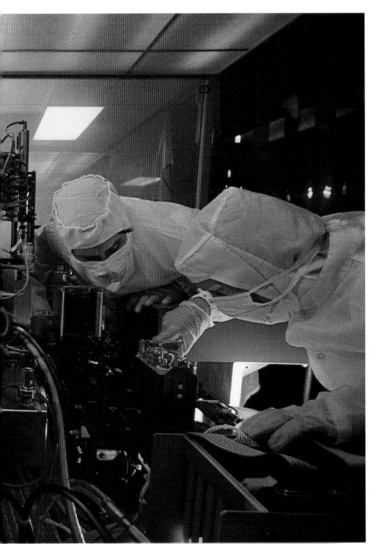

The legal regulations and codes of practice need to be matched to the specific materials and manual handling operations involved.

For example, if it were necessary for someone to carry a container full of a dangerous chemical across the factory floor, the following points would need to be considered:

▷ Is the weight of each full container acceptable for handling?
▷ Will the container lid be fastened securely?
▷ What type and level of protective clothing (e.g. overall, gloves, footware, etc.) will be needed?
▷ Is the container adequately marked with clear information about its contents and their hazardous nature?

If, however, water was being carried rather than toxic chemicals, the risk factor would be considerably lower and the safety precautions less rigorous.

As well as the legal requirements and more general codes of practice for health and safety, a considerable amount of documented information is available to help guide the design of safe products and working environments. Ergonomic studies and anthropometric data can be used to determine optimum positions for displays and controls on products and machines, and the most suitable sizes and arrangements for workspaces and conditions (e.g. distribution of light, noise, heating and ventilation).

It is an employer's responsibility to assess the risks involved in each stage of production and justify the level of precautions adopted to a Health and Safety Inspector.

# Production Schedules

*When all the elements of the manufacturing process have been considered and defined, production planning can begin. The step-by-step processes by which a product is going to be made need to be organised into the most efficient and cost-effective schedule.*

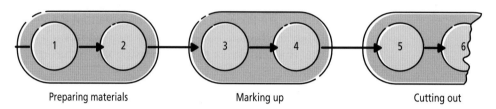

Preparing materials     Marking up     Cutting out

Begin by grouping the different stages of production together. Across these stages there are likely to be many sub-assemblies, i.e. groups of components and parts being assembled before they are added into the main production line.

When these operations have been identified, the next stage is to plan the layout of the production line. Often sub-assemblies are made in what are called manufacturing cells, which are smaller units of machines and operators.

When planning a production line, different operations can be coded by using different symbols.

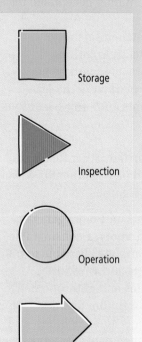

Storage

Inspection

Operation

Movement

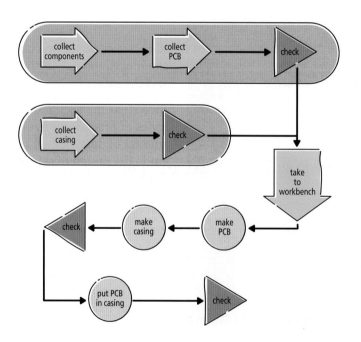

Other ways of organising production processes involve grouping similar machines and/or materials together in one area. This has some advantages, but generally increases the distances which components need to travel. A conveyor-belt approach is well suited to some types of product, but relies on a steady supply of parts and continuous operation: a delay or breakdown at any one stage can slow down or stop the whole system.

## Fine-Tuning Production

**Just In Time** is a material and production control system which ensures that materials and components arrive in the factory and at the assembly line just in time for the product to be made.

This helps eliminate excessive use of storage space and the possibility of running out of essential items. To achieve this, the factory type, factory layout, operation set-up time, work scheduling and production quality control all need to be considered.

The term can also be applied to the efficiency of delivery to a customer, at the right place at precisely the right time.

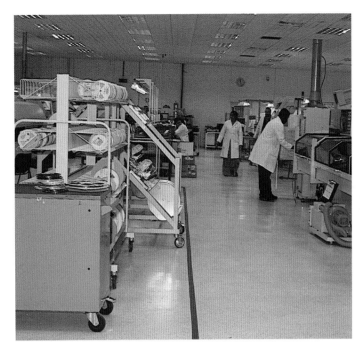

## Right On Schedule

In all types of manufacturing production, a complex and accurate production schedule is essential to tell the assemblers when to make and assemble all the different components.

**Critical path analysis** (or CPA) is a technique used for determining the overall schedule of a project. It involves defining the task, identifying its component stages and the order in which things need to be done, and estimating how long each operation is likely to take. A network path of the essential activities which must be completed before others can take place can then be created, and this provides an indication of the minimum amount of time which will be needed to schedule for production.

*A Gantt chart*

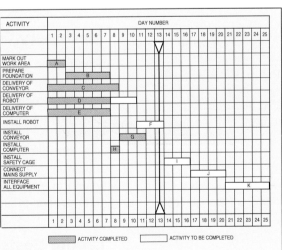

### IN YOUR PROJECT

▶ What operation is being carried out, and why? What alternatives might there be?

▶ Where is the operation done, and why? Where else might it be carried out?

▶ When is it done and why? When else might it be undertaken?

▶ Who carries it out, and why? Who else might do it?

▶ How is it undertaken, and why? How else might it be done?

▶ Remember that manufacturing is not just about making things, it is also about making them better – simpler, quicker, cheaper, more efficient, less damaging to the environment, etc.

# Making It Better

*How could you make your product simpler, quicker, cheaper and more efficient to manufacture? There are a number of specific aspects you can look at to achieve this.*

## Cutting costs to remain competitive

Price is increasingly a selling point for personal computers. Companies are forced to look for ways to cut costs to remain competitive. That means making small compromises on external features such as casing material and control-panel doors.

One company replaced its automatic floppy disc insert mechanism with a manual one, and started to use trackpads instead of trackballs on its portables because they cost less to make and service. They also started using plastic enclosures for its hard drives instead of more costly metal ones. Users accepted the changes fairly quickly. The company ran into problems, however, when they changed to a lightweight mouse from Malaysia that felt cheaply made. Users complained and they had to go back to a higher quality mouse.

Newer models have flimsier cases with plastic struts and flaps that easily break off. Even one of their service technicians has admitted that he's broken several such parts despite his training and experience.

Meanwhile a spokesperson for the company said that improving the technology and increasing the standards, not cutting corners, is how they plan to sell more computers. 'We absolutely do not believe that lowering the quality is the way to increase our sales', he says. 'Our brand is considered to be a high-quality product, and that's a good selling point for us.'

## IN YOUR PROJECT

▶ Keep the number of individual parts down to a minimum.
▶ 'Buy in' existing components and pre-assembled units (known as modules) wherever possible.
▶ Make components as similar as possible (e.g. all plastic or all metal, all curved or all rectangular). This will reduce the number of manufacturing processes and handling problems.
▶ Standardise components (e.g. use all one type of IC for logic functions) and use similar fixing methods in assembly.
▶ Avoid duplicating components by combining different parts of the circuit (e.g. a piezoelectric transducer can act as an input and output device).
▶ Purchase sections of the product from other suppliers pre-assembled.
▶ Keep the assembly process as simple as possible.
▶ Avoid machining and components that require fine tolerances (see pages 65 and 136). For example, a circuit with feedback can often function well with low-tolerance resistors and capacitors.

## Machinery Costs

Small batch manufacturing (see page 126) requires flexible machinery which can be retooled quickly and reprogrammed to produce new components. For example, a CNC milling machine can be used for short runs, up to about 1000 units. Large-scale production (e.g. 200 000 or more units) might use a dedicated injection moulding machine. The initial cost of the injection moulding tools is high but the unit cost of each item produced is significantly reduced.

## Labour Costs

A skilled CNC operator milling a limited number of shapes from plastic blanks will be expensive compared with an operator minding an injection moulding machine which is set up to automatically produce thousands of identical components for weeks. The scale of the production run determines the training, experience and cost of the labour involved.

# Final Testing and Evaluation

## Into Production

Give your final game or toy to some children and write notes on their reactions. Measure how long they played with it. What feature of the product seemed to hold their attention the most? This 'user trial' should enable you to describe areas of design which could be improved.

Show your product to a number of parents. Make brief notes on their comments. What reasons do they give for:

▷ considering buying the product;
▷ deciding they would not buy the product?

How long would you estimate the product will last in normal use? Drop the product from an increasing height and check it each time for damage. What type of warning may need to be put on the box about damage? What sort of liability will you accept if customers return damaged goods?

Is there any danger to the user, for example small parts that could choke a young child? Will you need a warning on the box, e.g. *'Warning! This product contains small parts. Unsuitable for ...'*?

While evaluating your electronic toy or game consider design issues such as safety, the use of recycleable materials and the efficiency of CAD/CAM production design methods. Don't forget to refer to your original specification. Support your comments by referring directly to the results of your testing.

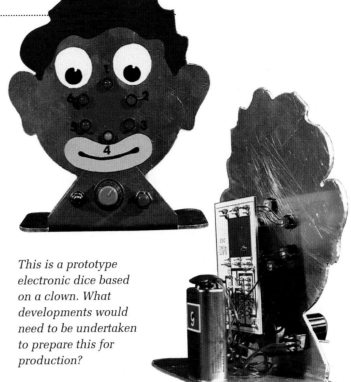

*This is a prototype electronic dice based on a clown. What developments would need to be undertaken to prepare this for production?*

Time how long it takes to make a small batch of three or four. Would another method of production have been quicker and therefore cheaper?

Move onto assembling the circuit boards, experimenting with different ways of organising the assembly. For example, what happens when each person:

▷ builds the whole board;
▷ takes a section to build and hands it on;
▷ adds just a few components and hands it on?

Who will check the quality of each indivdual's work, and when will it be done?

By timing the assembly with each method, make a written recommendation for the type of assembly line which should be set up.

▷ If you adopt a production line approach, how will you communicate to the other workers what they will do?
▷ Which method of production gave you the most satisfaction?
▷ Will workers' attitudes be important in the manufacturing process?

---

**IN YOUR PROJECT**

▶ Write a report on the advantages and disadvantages of the different production methods.
▶ Which would be the most suitable for your design? Justify your recommendation by referring to your experiments.

You could use a word processor to write your evaluation.

# Examination Questions

*You should spend about one and a half hours answering the following questions. To complete the paper you will need some plain A4 and A3 paper, basic drawing equipment, and colouring materials. You are reminded of the need for good English and clear presentation in your answers.*

**1. This question is about circuit board design and construction.** *(Total 7 marks)* See pages 132-133.

a) What do you understand by the term PCB? *(1 mark)*

b) When designing a PCB it is important to understand how the pins are numbered on ICs. How would you find pin 1 on an IC? *(2 marks)*

c) Draw an 8 pin IC to show how the other pins are numbered. *(2 marks)*

d) Explain two safety considerations when making a PCB. *(2 marks)*

**2. This question is about industrial practice.** *(Total 14 marks)* See pages 136-137.

In the past many electronic products have been housed in aluminium cases. They are now made from moulded plastic.

a) Name a suitable process and material that could now be used for the manufacture of a product case. *(2 marks)*

b) Explain two advantages of using this material and process. *(4 marks)*

c) Product cases are now designed on a CAD system. What do you understand by the term CAD? *(1 mark)*

d) What advantages are there when using a CAD system? *(2 marks)*

e) What must any manufacturer complete before it markets its products? *(2 marks)*

f) What do you understand by the terms quality control and quality assurance? *(3 marks)*

**3. This question is about PICs.** *(Total 18 marks)* See pages 118-119.

a) A PIC has to be used with other components to make in work. Name one of these components and describe what function it will perform. *(2 marks)*

b) What are the advantages and disadvantages of using a PIC in a product? *(4 marks)*

c) Draw the input part of a circuit that could be used with a PIC to sense when a switch is pressed off. *(2 marks)*

d) Draw the circuit diagram to show how a relay could connected to the PIC. Explain why a relay can not be directly connected to an output pin of a PIC. *(4 marks)*

e) Write a simple procedure to programme a PIC so it could operate six outputs as a dice. *(6 marks)*

## 4. This question is about counting. *(Total 11 marks)*
See pages 112-119.

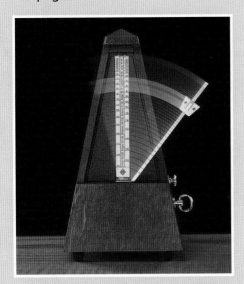

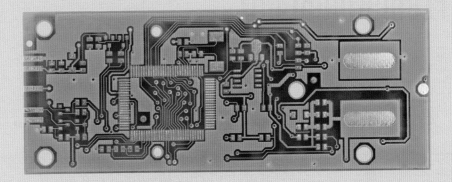

A company is going to manufacture an electronic metronome by combining an astable timer and decade counter.

- A small buzzer will sound on each beat.
- A 4017 IC is going to be used as the counter (see below)
- The final design will use one red LED to show the first beat and then a series of green LEDs to show the rest of the beats.

The manufacturer wants to be able to switch between 3 beats to 4 beats, after this the counter will go back the first beat and light the red LED.

a)  Draw the block diagram for the required system.  *(5 marks)*

b)  Complete the circuit above to show how the counter can be switched between 3 and 4 beats.  *(3 marks)*

c)  Show how the audible signal will be created by adding this to the circuit.  *(3 marks)*

```
           4017 IC Data
Pin   Function
1     output 5
2     output 1
3     output 0
4     output 2
5     output 6
6     output 7
7     output 3
8     0V
9     output 8
10    output 4
11    output 9
12    output ÷ 10
13    clock enable (0V)
14    clock (input)
15    reset
16    +V (3-15V)
```

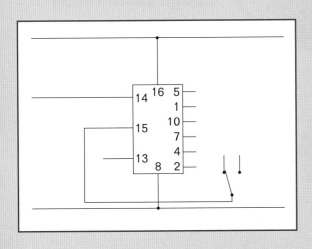

## 5. This question is about counting. *(Total 20 marks)*
See pages 112-117.

You have been asked to design a hand steady game that can be used at a local fair. Each competitor will be given three lives and a display must show how many lives the competitor has lost.

a)  The input part of the system will use a debounced switch. What do you understand by the term debounced switch and why is it needed in the system? Draw the circuit diagram for the final input part of the system.  *(6 marks)*

b)  It has been decided to use a seven segment display to show the number of lives the competitor has lost. Describe how this component can display different numbers.  *(2 marks)*

c)  A seven-segment display can not be connected directly to the input part of the system. What process component must be used with the display? Draw the final circuit diagram for the seven segment display and its process component.  *(6 marks)*

d)  You could use three LEDs to show the lost lives and a PIC in the final design. Give three other features that could be included in the design and say how they could be used.

*(6 marks)*

**Total marks = 70**

# Promotional Gift

Manufacturing PCBs (page 132)

Choosing a Switch (page 68)

Power Supplies (page 94)

PROMOTIONAL GIFT

Logic Gates (page 42)

Joining Circuits (page 72)

*An international chain of business and leisure hotels wants to offer a promotional gift to guests visiting hotels within the group. They would like to provide a simple electronic device which would illuminate a watch during the night if a guest wanted to know the time.*

## The Task

You have been asked to develop a proposal which will:

▷ hold a range of watches at an angle that allows the face to be seen easily when the user is lying down in bed;
▷ include a method of illuminating the watch to be operated by a simple touch switch (a time delay on the light would be a worthwhile additional feature);
▷ be relatively cheap to produce but should have a 'quality' feel;
▷ include the hotel chain's name and logo. This should be a permanent and clearly visible feature.

## Investigation

You will need to undertake some careful research before you start designing.

▷ What angle should the watch be held at? Check the height of bedside cabinets in relation to bed heights. Perhaps the angle should be adjustable.
▷ How much light is needed to illuminate the watc face?
▷ What is a suitable period of time for the light source to remain on? Experiment and record you findings.

You will need to study a variety of men's and women's watches, and also the types of straps and fastenings used. Record your findings, including accurate measurements.

how long will light stay on?

is watch held at the correct angle?

will the stand fall over?

## Design Specification

From the conclusions to your research you will need to write a specification which defines the requirements for the watch stand in terms of:

▷ the minimum and maximum size;
▷ the 'lighting' time;
▷ the most suitable materials;
▷ for how long the item is expected to last;
▷ the target manufacturing cost.

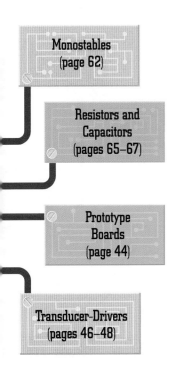

Monostables
(page 62)

Resistors and
Capacitors
(pages 65–67)

Prototype
Boards
(page 44)

Transducer-Drivers
(pages 46–48)

## Developing the Electronics

### Inputs

What sort of switch would be most suitable, e.g. a push switch or perhaps a touch switch (see page 68)?

If you decide to make a touch switch, what form will it take? Could you use copper tape to make a pair of contacts (see page 51)?

### Delays

Look at the monostable circuits on pages 62 to 64. You will need to work out the delay by selecting the appropriate resistor/capacitor values (see page 67). Could you combine the input and delay circuits to reduce the number of components (see page 70)?

| Input Switch | → | Process Monostable | → | Output Bulb/LED |

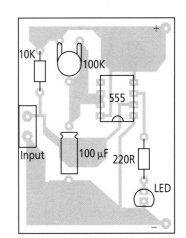

### Outputs

Will a bulb or LED be best to light the watch face? Make up a circuit and test it. Which works best – a bulb or LED? What about battery life?

### Power supply

Depending on the output, you will need to select a power supply. Remember – the battery could be the largest component you have to house in the product. Pages 94-95 have useful information on power supplies.

## Developing the Product

Use a suitable prototyping system to test the circuit you have designed. Does the delay match your calculations? You may need to change the resistor/capacitor values to achieve the exact time delay you require.

The electronic components will need to be soldered together on a circuit board (see pages 51-53).

When you have got the electronics well developed you should be able to put some overall dimensions on your product. A cardboard model will help you finalise some of the details (see page 97).

You will need to consider the following things:

▷ Which components need to be easily accessible for the user?
▷ Should they be in the same compartment as the battery?
▷ Can the product be assembled easily?
▷ What materials will it be made from?
▷ What methods of manufacture will be used?

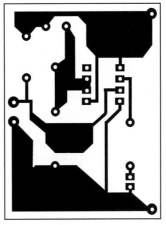

## Planning and Making It!

Plan carefully the making of the final product. You might find it easier to add some features to the component parts before assembly. The chosen finish should only be applied after you have completed all the making. Don't forget – any blemishes on the surface of the model will show through a paint finish.

## Final Testing and Evaluation

Test the product out yourself and ask others to evaluate it.

▷ Does the light illuminate the watch clearly?
▷ Does the light stay on long enough?
▷ Is it easy to find the switch in the dark?
▷ Is it stable?
▷ What percentage of watches does the product hold?

Record your findings and make any proposals for improving the product. Remember to use sketches as well as notes in your evaluation.

# Electronic Body Adornment

**Project Suggestions**

*Design a range of jewellery items which incorporate electronics, aimed at a teenage market. Make at least one of the items and explain how a small batch could be manufactured as cheaply as possible.*

*Your solution should be lively and amusing and act as a talking point.*

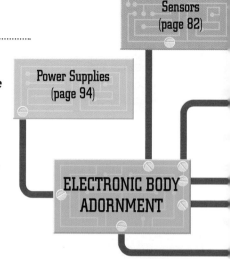

Sensors
(page 82)

Power Supplies
(page 94)

**ELECTRONIC BODY ADORNMENT**

Traditional jewellery involves the use of precious and semi-precious metals and stones. However, modern and cheaper materials such as plastics have now gained acceptance. Your solution should use low-cost materials and components in imaginative and unexpected ways.

## Investigation

Find pictures of jewellery from different cultures and different times. Look out for examples of unusual traditional or contemporary body adornment. Prepare a number of spreads to record what you discover.

Make a study of some existing items of body adornment. What are they made from? How do they fit a range of body sizes? Find out what teenagers look for when choosing jewellery.

Gather together a range of materials you might be able to use, such as acrylic, copper, aluminium, wood, paper and fibre. Comment on their qualities and suitability.

Don't forget to consider 'found' materials such as packaging, ribbon, cable, plastic components, etc.

Experiment with the materials by re-forming, cutting, joining and changing their surface appearance to develop a series of interesting shapes, forms, textures and colours.

How might the electronic components become a visible and decorative part of the design?

## Design Specification

From the conclusions to your research you will need to write a specification which defines the requirements for the range of items and the electronics in terms of:

▷ safety requirements;
▷ the maximum sizes and weights for each piece;
▷ the most suitable materials;
▷ for how long the items are expected to last;
▷ the target selling price.

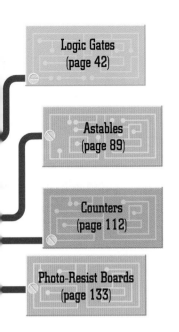

Logic Gates
(page 42)

Astables
(page 89)

Counters
(page 112)

Photo-Resist Boards
(page 133)

## Developing the Electronics

### Inputs

The inputs could include simple touch or membrane switches. Remember that size and weight will be important. What else might activate the process (see page 82)?

### Process

An astable circuit will give a pulsed signal to an output or outputs (see page 89). Flashing LEDs provide a process and output in one. What difference will there be if they are connected in series or parallel?

Dedicated ICs such as a random output generator or LED chaser, and music/sound effect generator chips are a very good way of reducing the size and weight of the electronics.

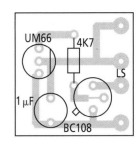

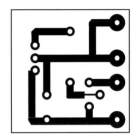

### Outputs

These could include LEDs, bulbs and piezo transducers. You will need to take into account the size and weight of these components.

### Power supplies

The battery will have to be small and light, perhaps a button type. How will it be connected and held? An alternative might be a separate battery and lead (see page 94).

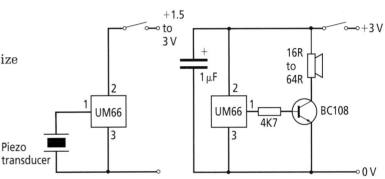

*Circuit for musical effect chip*

## Developing the Product

You will need to finalise the design for the mask and make the pcb circuit.

Make and test prototypes regularly to check that your jewellery is:

▷ comfortable to wear and eye-catching;
▷ electronically reliable.

*How suitable are your designs for batch production? Would they need to be made differently?*

## Making It!

Plan carefully how you will make a final high quality version of one of your designs. Work with care and accuracy, and ensure you achieve a very high standard of finish.

If two or more people worked together, how could the manufacturing process be speeded up? Would the design need to be changed?

## Final Testing and Evaluation

Choose a suitable social occasion. Wear your design yourself or ask someone else to.

▷ How do others respond to your jewellery? Does their response match your expectations?
▷ How keen are people to own a piece of your electronic jewellery?
▷ Was your product robust enough to survive the evening?

# Alarm Around the Home

*There are many locations around the home where an alarm would be useful. An example would be a device that warns you if the fridge door is left open.*

Manufacturing With Other Materials (page 124)

Quality Counts (page 132)

## The Task

A manufacturer of electronic products has asked you to identify a situation in the home that requires an alarm. You should then design and make a working prototype which could be used for market testing and later developed for mass production.

## Investigation

You will need to look in all the rooms around your home and identify places where an alarm could be used. Protecting young children against harm from chemicals or the road are important areas to look at and can warn parents of potential accidents. Here are some ideas to get you started. Alarms could be used on the:

▷ fridge and cleaning cupboard in the kitchen
▷ medicine cupboard in the bathroom
▷ CD collection in your bedroom, as your brother uses them without asking
▷ door of the garden shed
▷ garden gate.

Some of the alarms need to go off as soon as they are triggered. Others, such as the fridge alarm, need to have a delay in them. Once the alarm has been triggered it needs to stay on. This is called a latch. You can use a thyristor as a latch. You can find out more about thyristors on page 86.

You will need to measure the door and frame of where the alarm is going to be placed.

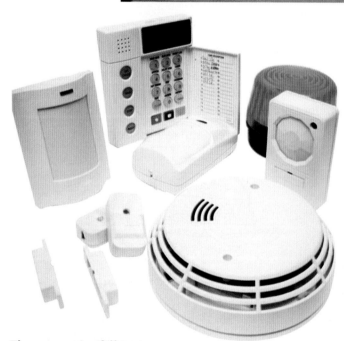

*There are many different types of household alarm devices. Which would be the most appropriate for this project?*

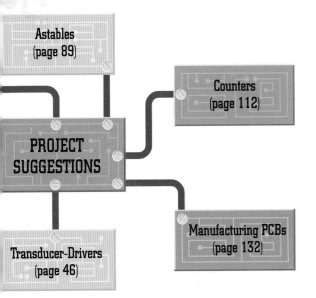

**Astables**
(page 89)

**Counters**
(page 112)

**PROJECT SUGGESTIONS**

**Manufacturing PCBs**
(page 132)

**Transducer-Drivers**
(page 46)

## Developing the Product

Model the operation of your system before you make it. Use a set of system boards or prototype board to test your circuit before you make a PCB. The appearance of your final design must fit in with the style of the room. It will need to be robust and easy to install. You will need to power the circuit and also replace the battery when it runs down. Your device would also need a test button to check its operation.

## Designing the System

You must be able to switch the alarm on. This is called enabling or arming the alarm. You could use a key switch. Sensitive systems such as movement detectors will also need to have a time delay before they arm themselves. You will need an input sensor that will trigger the alarm. This could be a reed switch, LDR or microswitch.

The output needs to be an intermittent audible alarm.

| Input | Control | Output |
|---|---|---|
| Arming switch | Latch | Astable |
| Sensor | | Buzzer |

You can also use a relay as a latch.

## Planning and Making It!

You could vacuum-form a case or use sheet material. The pieces will need to be glued together and finished to match the room's appearance. The size and layout of the case will need to hold all the system's components securely.

*Avoid a jumble!*

## Final Testing and Evaluation

Choose a suitable location in your house and test the operation of your product. Ask someone else to try it as well.

▷ Is it reliable and robust?
▷ Can it be cleaned?
▷ Can the alarm be heard outside the room?
▷ Does the design fit the appearance of the room?

How could you modify your design so it could be mass produced? Consider different manufacturing processes and how you can reduce costs.

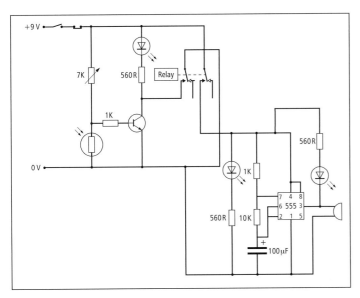

*A light sensitive circuit, with a latch and astable output.*

# Index